$#47\frac{00}{}$

?B
st
1le
&
ned

The Calculus of Intimacy

The Calculus of Intimacy

A Teaching Life

Richard J. Murphy, Jr.

For Gregg —
with affection & long-standing
thanks!
Rich - 7/09

Ohio State University Press
Columbus

Earlier versions of chapters 4, 7, and 10 appeared in *English Education* 23 (October 1991): 178–87; *College Composition and Communication* 40 (December 1989): 466–72; and *College English* 52 (December 1990): 898–903.

Parts of chapter 3 appeared in different form in "Polanyi and Composition: A Personal Note on a Human Science," in *Into the Field: Sites of Composition Studies*, ed. Anne Ruggles Gere (New York: Modern Language Association, 1993), 72–83. Parts of chaper 13 appeared in "Kata," *Virginia English Bulletin* 39 (Fall 1989): 42–46.

Library of Congress Cataloging-in-Publication Data

Murphy, Richard John, 1945–
The calculus of intimacy: a teaching life / Richard J. Murphy, Jr.
p.   cm.
Includes bibliographical references (p.).
ISBN 0–8142–0611–5 (alk. paper).—ISBN 0–8142–0612–3 (pbk.: alk. paper)
1. College teaching—United States—Psychological aspects.
2. Teacher-student relationships. Intimacy (Psychology).
I. Title.
LB2331. M84 1993   93–2555
378.1'25—dc20   CIP

Text and jacket design by Bruce Gore, Gore Studios.
Type set in Sabon.
Printed by Cushing-Malloy, Ann Arbor, MI.

Printed in the U.S.A.
9 8 7 6 5 4 3 2 1

For Susie

Imagination . . . manifests the essence by breaking the prestige of fact. In imagining another state of affairs or another kingdom, I perceive the possible, and in the possible, the essential.

> Paul Ricoeur
> *Fallible Man*

I'm producing too many stories at once because what I want is for you to feel, around the story, a saturation of other stories that I could tell and maybe will tell or who knows may already have told on some other occasion, a space full of stories that perhaps is simply my lifetime . . .

> Italo Calvino
> *If on a winter's night a traveler*

Was there no safety? No learning by heart of the ways of the world? No guide, no shelter, but all was miracle, and leaping from the pinnacle of a tower into the air?

> Virginia Woolf
> *To the Lighthouse*

Our knowledge of life is a sharing of life—a reliving.

> Michael Polanyi
> *Knowing and Being*

Contents

Prologue

The Calculus of Intimacy

Teresa Simpson submitted an essay in my Freshman English class one February. The paper told a story about herself. Her mother had died when Teresa was very young; her father had never remarried. Teresa had grown up among photographs of her mother that her dad kept in a family album in the living room and on the walls of the stairway down to the basement. Others would say—her aunt, for example, and her cousins—that Teresa looked like her mom. The older she got the more people would remark that they were growing alike. Teresa had a graduation portrait done at Foss Studios in the mall in Warrenton, with her charcoal sweater and a string of pearls. Everyone who had known her mother said, "Shoot, Teresa, you look just like her."

Teresa did not think so. Neither did her dad (or so he said), but sometimes she would catch him looking at her sideways. She would be at the sink washing the dishes, and he would walk into the kitchen from the dining room with some dirty glasses and before he had set them down on the counter, before he would get even halfway across the room sometimes, he would stop and just look at her, at the light on her red hair, at the slope of her neck and shoulders. Sometimes, Teresa would hear him stop, would sense him looking at her, and she would half turn with her hands still soapy up to her elbows and catch him just the instant before he looked away.

At the end of the paper, Teresa pasted two photographs— one, an instant glossy, the date still printed clearly in blue by

1

Fotomat, "July 16, 1970," of her mother standing in the sun on the sidewalk outside their duplex apartment holding Teresa as a baby; the second picture, below it, the graduation portrait of Teresa herself in sweater and pearls.

I was moved by all of this—the gesture of trust in me with which Teresa had included the irreplaceable photographs, the complex insight with which she had written a paper that touched both her father's desire and her own. I gave her an A on it (sometimes I can grade without an instant of hesitation), and when we talked later about it in my office, Teresa told me she had hoped for an A. She had never written a paper like that, she said, but when it was done, she knew it was good, and she hoped I would like it.

She sat in the wooden chair at the corner of my desk. I can see her there vividly still—shrunk inside her bulky navy blue winter coat, so small her feet barely touched the floor, her red hair disordered by the way she ran her hand through it nervously, sitting there in the office of her professor. I looked at her sideways. She did not want to be, you know, conceited or anything, she told me, but she sort of knew it was good. And then, because she knew I understood (or hoped I did), she laughed.

This is a book about teaching. Its immediate subject is the teaching of writing to new college students in required courses often called Freshman English. But I cannot even begin to talk about that without my subject's enlarging. I cannot limit it to college teaching or Freshman English. It includes teaching, learning, and writing more generally. Yet these will not do either. They are too ambitious. They implode: like Teresa, I am writing about myself.

I have been teaching for nearly twenty-five years. I subscribe to the *New Yorker*, the *American Scholar*, several journals of the National Council of Teachers of English, and the *New York Review of Books*. For a hundred miles along the Appalachian Trail, I hike in the rain with my son Kevin's Boy Scout troop, and before sleep on the floor of the rustic shelter, I write in my journal by candlelight. My wife, Susie, and I order decaffeinated coffee at McDonald's and edit drafts of her review articles for the *Journal of Reading*. My desk is piled with books; so are the shelves in the living room, boxes in the basement, the nightstand next to my bed, still more coming in the mail, books I will never have time to read. We've stopped taking any newspaper. I sit dumbly in front of the television, squeezing the remote control channel scanner, and let America pour over me in bits like a shower massage. When I think about teaching, learning, and writing, I cannot separate them from the person engaged in these acts.

And I do not want to.

In the current national debate about school reform, issues like literacy, curriculum revision, test results, and teacher certification are framed abstractly. Knowledge is usually listed with scant reference to knowers. Skills are defined outside the context of real classrooms. The Rand Corporation releases study after study describing legislative initiatives to improve public schooling while classroom teachers continue to collect lunch money and assign penalty hall and judge the growth of bean plants in school science fairs.

The situation is very similar in college. Though some disputes get a wide public hearing—such as the one at Stanford University over the content of the basic course in civilization—most college teachers are unaffected by canon quarrels. Even the deep (and probably unanswerable) question of whether colleges ought to place a higher value on undergraduate teaching or on research has little effect on the personal character of a professor's work. It certainly influences her choices—whether to make extra time for students or to lecture and hold office hours and then disappear into lab or library; whether to assign new readings in her courses or rely on old (and already well-annotated) standbys; whether to give essay examinations (and thus commit herself to days of reading and evaluating them) or computer-scored objective tests. Whatever her choices, they are always personal, and the college professor teaches—like all teachers everywhere—with memory and some peculiar distillation of hope.

My neighbor came over to my porch last week at dusk to tell me her son was home from college for the summer. It took a while for him to unpack, she said, to ease his way back into the house that had closed behind him when he left. Judy thought that maybe some of his stuff was still in the trunk of his car, as if he were uncertain whether to be a guest or to reestablish residency. But one night as she was getting ready for bed, he came into her room with a sheaf of papers. Things he'd written during the year at school. Maybe she'd like to look at them? She would, and did, every page, every word.

"You teachers have an amazing effect," she told me. "Dan wrote things in those papers he'd never said, things I never knew he thought. It's like that girl you spoke about . . ." She reminded me that she had heard me tell Teresa's story. "In some ways you get closer to them than their parents ever can."

Yes. Or their lovers. Or their friends. Sometimes it is a deep intimacy, unlike any other, purer than a priest's or a therapist's, less disinterested than either.

The Carnegie Foundation for the Advancement of Teaching has been studying teachers lately in the apparent hope of making systematic academic reform acknowledge our felt experience. I am glad to see that. No other plan will work. But even the Carnegie approach is compromised. Its survey asks reasonable questions, provides measurable answers. Its results are statistically unobjectionable. But what questionnaire will capture the current of our work as teachers?

My daughter was born with a defective heart. Every year now she is tested by cardiologists who monitor its strength and rhythm. For an entire day, she wears a battery-powered box strapped in a leather case on her hip, wired to her chest, wrist, and back. She sleeps with it, hides it as well as she can under loose sweatshirts, brings it everywhere (whether to class or cheerleading practice), and keeps a timed log of her activities. The box is a portable electrocardiogram, a Holter Monitor. Were its record printed out (instead of being read by a computer) it would consume one hundred yards of EKG tape each hour. It traces the continuous beat of her heart. That is the sort of thing researchers or policymakers need who wish to understand our work as teachers, an electrocardiogram of our lives.

My inclination to inquire into the personal in teaching is reinforced by what I teach. The official subject of Freshman English is "expository writing." But its actual subject is reading and writing, and more than those: thinking, and more even than that: living. I do not mean it is my business to teach students how they should live. I mean that when they think about how to read and write, they *are* thinking about living. Even if I wished to distance myself more, to view what I do as a job rather than a profession, my students' work would keep reminding me.

Brett Trahan waited after class the first day of one semester to say he was a math major and that he would probably drop the 8:00 A.M. literature class I was teaching. The next day he stopped to tell me he had decided to stay. Every morning he was there, near the back of the fifth row, solid, trim, concentrated, his red hair shaved short. I imagined he was a wrestler or a swimmer. At the end of the course, he waited again, until everyone else was gone. He began elliptically. "That story by D. H. Lawrence. 'The Odor of Chrysanthemums'. . ." Standing with his feet apart, balanced, braced, his high school letter jacket hooked on two fingers over his shoulder, he looked down and paused as if lost.

Then he started over: "I wrote a story. I thought it was pretty good. Then I read Lawrence. Just the first paragraph, and I knew."

"What did you know?"

"How paltry mine was. How much a paragraph could say. Every word. Even the silence."

We looked at each other. I remembered Lawrence's withering chrysanthemums and the fiery dusk at his coal pits and the loneliness. We were silent. I cannot know for sure what Brett was thinking, but I imagined he wanted me to realize the story was about him. I supposed he hoped I would understand.

"Yes," I said.

The American Association of Higher Education has embarked on a project to examine and improve college teaching. They have not begun with prescriptions for reform; instead they are asking us what we do and what we think it means. It is a good place to start. At a seminar convened for college teachers, AAHE invited participants to talk with one another about their teaching experience, to say what they can usually find no place for in their resumes or annual professional activity reports.

I am thankful for this approach. It recognizes that our stories of our own practice affect everything: our purposes and commitments, our ability to reflect on what we do, our desire to learn, our willingness to change. It assumes, as psychologist Jerome Bruner has maintained, that in the stories we construct of our lives we define ourselves. It admits, too, the felt experience of our work: that at the center of the mundane lies the intimate.

Peter Clarke was six feet tall. He weighed maybe two hundred pounds, still mostly muscle. His ordinary dress for class was jeans, a torn black T-shirt, and a seasoned leather bomber jacket. During the semester, his hair grew. He started pulling it back into a ponytail, so the small gold earring in his left ear was exposed. Many days he came to class with a limp and a scab on his forehead or cheek, as if recovering from a fight.

Peter was wasting his time in Freshman English. Not doing the writing, not doing it carefully. He said he was concerned about his grade, but so far he had not been doing much about it. He was on his way to a D in the course. He had not completed all the work. What he had was too short, too misdirected. I had been gradually losing confidence in his ability or willingness. I thought perhaps he was distracted by the extraordinary challenges of freshman year in college. Perhaps he was troubled by problems with his roommate, worries from home, difficulty in his other courses . . . I didn't know what.

But he met with me in my office to discuss a paper. He began (as I usually ask students to begin) by reading to me, and the first lines went like this:

> When I first saw the old house I was overwhelmed by its charm.
> Not the kind of charm an adult would see but the kind a child
> would see. I didn't notice the beautifully handcrafted bannister
> that followed the old spiral staircase; I noticed the rafters in the
> attic that were high enough to hang a swing from. I didn't see the
> rock fences that outlined the huge backyard or the blackberry
> patch surrounded by pear and cherry trees; I saw the swamp in
> the middle of one of the cow fields that was ideal for catching
> tadpoles and minnows. The two giant shade trees in the front
> yard weren't just shade trees but climbing trees with great poten-
> tial for forts. This, I thought, is going to be a great place to live.

On and on it went, remembering the features of the place—
the porch, the staircase, the railings, the country setting with

fields for walks with his sister and father, the terrors of that door on the staircase landing the landlords kept ominously locked.

I cheered as he read, could not contain myself. "Yes," I said when he described the annoyance he felt that he had to sleep with his sister. "Yes," I said to the image of him sleeping with his head next to the attic door, one eye open for the monsters that would descend in the dark. I laughed and sang with delight at his writing, at his doing it, at his knowing how good it was, at his comments along the way (neither of us would let him read it all the way through without interruption; both of us stopped to comment as he went). The thing was that he *knew* what he was doing.

It had happened all of a sudden; finally, two-thirds of the way through the semester he had become (perhaps for the first time in his life) a student. School made sense to him there for the moment. He understood.

This is not an unmixed story. School is not an unmixed place. When Peter had finished reading, I told him that I thought his paper was simply excellent. And then I remembered that he had brought a draft of the essay to class to read to a group of his fellow students. It was an unpromising meeting. They sat in the corner giggling and elbowing each other like seventh-graders and looking conspiratorial. I had gone back to talk with them, to ask some questions I thought would help them focus on their drafts.

"What did the group think of your paper?" I asked Peter.

"You want to know the truth?" he said. "I didn't read it to them. I didn't want to risk it. I didn't think they'd like it. I didn't think they'd understand."

I told him I knew what he meant. His whole body jerked in the chair. "You do?"

"Yes," I said, "I think so. It's hard to share such things . . ." Peter took over my sentence: ". . .You don't want to let on that you care about them." And as he finished speaking, he waved his ponytail and settled his big body back into the chair.

A friend wrote to me about a student in a Freshman English course of hers. He was quiet, withdrawn behind a natural reserve and the thick veil of curls that usually hung over his eyes.

She was put off by him, thought the collection of earrings he wore decadent and ugly, but his work was excellent. Papers on *Sir Gawain and the Green Knight* and "The Masque of the Red Death," on Margaret Mead and vegetarianism, all of them she found boldly independent. Just once he wore his hair up, on a visit to her office. They drank coffee, listened to Albinoni, talked. He held the cup in both hands, sipping nervously. Boldness and nervousness—it is their mixture in that moment that my friend remembers. It reminded her of herself. His hands on the coffee cup were like hers, she wrote to me. The day she read in the newspaper of his arrest for drug possession, it was the image of those hands that came back to her. She imagined the handcuffs, and she felt them tighten on her own wrists.

When we talk publicly about teaching—when we conceptualize and analyze it, when we develop programs for training teachers and tests for assessing them, when we blueprint school reforms that teachers will be the ones to put into practice—we need to remind ourselves of just what a complicated and intimate act teaching is. The more closely we look, the more we will see. Of classrooms and offices, libraries and books. Syllabi and grade report sheets. And always persons—teachers and students, parents and children—their transactions in motion, the lines between them blurring.

The bureaucracy of school is in the business of measurement. Everything is quantified: FTEs (the number of students enrolled full time), test scores, clerical supplies, class sizes, instructional days, recertification hours. How can the work of school be reported if it cannot be numbered? But the entire apparatus of numbers is in place in order to foster an immeasurable event: the personal meeting of teacher and student. This is an unwelcome irony to those who want schools accountable and who hope to correct the system by systematizing it further. But the truth is that the essential act of school is, in the terms we are accustomed to using, incalculable.

One semester I decided to write a term paper for students in my Freshman English class, not as a model exactly, but as a text to observe, study, and criticize. As it turned out, the paper was of little use to them but very valuable to me. My general subject was Isaac Newton, and my brief research was full of surprises. Though I had studied eighteenth-century England in graduate school, I knew very little about the man or his career. I did not know, for example, that he invented calculus (what he called originally "the method of fluxions") or that he fought bitterly for decades with Gottfried Leibniz over credit for the discovery. I did not know how he devised calculus, or why, or what sorts of problems his new method was first used to help solve.

In mathematics classes in school, calculus had always baffled me. Arithmetic, algebra, geometry, trig—those I managed fine. I could accept them as abstract systems. I understood (at least functionally) their relations and operations. But approaching calculus, I had balked. I was unable to comprehend quantities in the process of change, numbers that were not fixed. Reading about Newton, however, in biography and history permitted me to glimpse for the first time the theoretical and practical problems that calculus helped clarify. What are the paths of celestial bodies orbiting each other at changing speeds? What is the direction of a beam of light when it reflects off the curved surface of a lens? At what angle of elevation will a cannon hurl a ball the farthest distance? How can the area of a complex figure—created by, say, irregularly curved lines—be approximated?

I think we need an invention like Newton's to allow us to understand teaching. We need a calculus of intimacy. The acts of teaching and learning are dynamic. The area of our work is bounded by lines in motion. At any one moment, it is very difficult to plot the curve of our path, to say where we have been or where we are going. I cannot predict what the new calculus would be, but I am reasonably certain it would not be mathematical. I suspect that it would be closer to narrative, to the story of the self in flux.

Montaigne said, "I am myself the matter of my book." Teachers in America—like those in the AAHE seminar—are beginning to be encouraged to tell their own stories, too. It is a treacherous undertaking for reasons everyone knows. The self is incorrigibly biased. Autobiographers often tell different tales than they intend. Life remembered is as much fiction as fact.

But, granting these liabilities, I think policymakers need to include the self-portrait of teachers in their thinking about schools. We teachers need it as well, the self of our own stories, in order to understand the nature not only of our work, but of our lives.

1

New

MY OFFICE IN Young Hall at Radford University is directly across the corridor from the classroom in which I most often teach. The windows on one side of the narrow brick rectangular building view the lawns of Muse Quad. The windows on the other look over a parking lot of pin oak trees and across the New River. Administrative offices occupy the first floor, but the upper three stories are devoted to faculty offices and classrooms, each floor divided between the two. The design connects. It brings teachers and students together, creates an architectural link between classrooms and offices. When the class hour ends, the talk can continue across the hall.

I like this plan. It has a lot to recommend it. I have taught in many other buildings with different arrangements: offices and classrooms on different floors; no offices at all, just classrooms, faculty offices in another building. Many different ways to separate teachers and students have been built into the design of academic buildings. But Young Hall was drawn by planners with the desire to bring teachers and students together. Both the desire and the plan were good.

Today I am standing in the doorway of Young 405, the room where my Freshman English class will meet Tuesday morning. The room is empty, the hall still. The school year has not yet begun. The floor is mottled-beige vinyl tile, buffed to a lustre. The ceiling is high, fifteen feet up, covered in textured acoustic stucco and suspending five white fluorescent light fixtures. The walls on three sides are pale yellow concrete block.

11

Across the front of the room stretches a black chalkboard. A bulletin board hangs on the side wall near the one door.

A bare room, free of decoration. Since classes rotate here every school day, no teacher considers it his or her own. A teacher who props a print of Turner's *Snowstorm in the Alps* on the aluminum chalk ledge does not leave it in the room. A class displaying their collaborative writing projects for each other will tape them to the walls at the beginning of class and more often than not take them down again at the end. Many faculty consider it a courtesy to erase the chalkboard before they leave the room, and they expect their colleagues to do the same. What will remain, once the year gets going, are occasional signs in the upper right-hand corner of the board—"Yearbooks At Heth Student Center $15.00 *Please do not erase.*" "Found: purple umbrella. Ask in Young 402."—and advertisements posted on the bulletin board for discount magazine subscriptions and Christmas ski trip packages to Innsbruck or Kitzbühel.

Though the fire marshal's plate over the light switch declares the room's capacity to be fifty-three, I count seventy-one desks today, steel and plastic, eight rows, nine desks in all except the row by the windows. Some teachers rearrange the desks for their classes, pulling them all into one huge approximation of a circle, though it's almost impossible to create such a circle without leaving some clutter of empty desks in the middle. Sometimes teachers ask students to group themselves in threes or fours. The furniture never quite gets back to its regular order during the day. In the winter, wet umbrellas, mud, and slush-edged boots make a mess of the floor. But every morning, whatever the season, thanks to the silent ministrations of the housekeeping night crew, the room is fresh and ready for the day.

Our university meetings were yesterday, all day, department and college meetings in the morning, then the faculty convocation in the afternoon addressed by the president. Tonight—Saturday—there will be a banquet welcoming the faculty back to another school year. Monday will be devoted to late registration. Classes begin Tuesday.

Then the hall here in Young will be jammed. Old friends

and classmates dressed in summer's limes and pinks will try to resist the current of passing students, hugging on the move, spinning around, backstepping, bumping into strangers, greeting each other on their way to and from classes. When pulled apart, they will call out their new phone numbers to each other over the heads of other students. Freshmen will be rechecking their computerized class schedules to make sure they are in the right building. They do not want to get lost on the very first day of class, walk into the wrong room, have to leave with everybody watching them.

One fall semester, a student sat through the entire first class, then handed me back the syllabus. "Math," she said. "I was looking for Math 101." She had endured seventy-five minutes of Introduction to Expository Writing rather than walk out quietly in front of everyone after a minute and a half. Few students know that teachers get lost, too, but we do. First day of the term, the instructor walks in briskly, writes his name on the board, passes out the syllabi, waits for the students to read. He is all business. At last, one student timidly asks if this is English 101, section 67.

"No," the instructor answers, easily, benevolently. "This is section 68."

Heads shake in unison. Huh? . . . Professor lurches. Does anyone have a class schedule? Twenty hands go up. He hardly scans the newsprint page before he is retrieving his syllabi, erasing the board, straightening his spine, and smiling his way out the door.

The hall on Tuesday will be full of "How was your summer?" Cool. A lotta fun. Pretty boring; I just worked and tried to save some money. Yeah, mine too. Did you get to the beach? Formulaic answers, but sung out with such enthusiasm that the singers' affection for each other will be unmistakable, and their gladness at being back.

The new students in my class will be from all over Virginia, some from beyond, many of them from small towns. Galax, Martinsville, Watsonville, Martinez, some small town, somewhere. Even if their homes are in Washington or San Francisco, on Tuesday they will feel small town. This is it. College.

Later Colleen will write about it or tell me about it when we talk together in my office about one of her papers. Her best friend from high school was going to come to Radford, too. They were going to room together, they said, and they talked and talked about what it would be like, shopped, dreamed about matching covers for their beds, planned to combine their sound systems. But in the end, the friend did not come, so Colleen is assigned a roommate she does not know in a room that looks like nowhere she has ever imagined. Narrow, long enough on each side for one twin bed frame and a wooden desk, one window at the end of the room opposite the door, yellow paint, a single light fixture in the center of the ceiling. It is the most desolate place she has ever been.

I imagine her arrival. Colleen and her dad and mother and grandmother drive up together pulling the U-Haul. They inch into Radford from Interstate 81 in a caravan of other arriving students, drive around looking for a parking place, and finally pull onto the grass under the trees on the Tyler Avenue median strip. Colleen's dorm is Muse Hall, eleven stories tall on the corner of Norwood Street. They find the door, then the elevator, then the ninth floor.

"*Well . . . ,*" her dad says with a rush of breath after they have taken one turn around the barren room. "Here you *are.*" He claps his hands together and heads down to the car for the first load of stuff. For just a moment, Colleen stays behind. Sits down on the striped mattress. Gets up to look out the window at the Norfolk and Southern railroad tracks, the ruined brick smokestack in a field of straw weeds, the brown river, the delivery bay behind the dorm dining room. She tells herself not to cry.

I know that delivery bay: I park there during the faculty banquet at the beginning of each year. And the tracks: I drive across them on my way down to the Dedmon Center, to swim or do some Nautilus exercise. One Saturday when my younger son, Stephen, was only three or four, he and I explored the smokestack, picking our way through the weeds, climbing over piles of broken brick to look inside and up. Across the shadows, from mortar cracks in the old walls, ran lines of surprising light.

I came to Radford in the fall of 1979.

My first teaching job had been at Moreau, a private Catholic high school in Hayward, California. I stayed there for two years, 1968–70, teaching English and Latin to ninth-, tenth-, and eleventh-graders, and coaching the speech club. During the summer of 1970, I taught sixth-grade reading and arithmetic at St. Louis Bertrand's School in east Oakland. As a graduate student in English at the University of California, Berkeley, I was appointed to several assistantships, first as a reader in two large undergraduate lecture courses in 1972, then as an assistant teacher in three small Freshman English courses in 1973 and 1974. I taught two Freshman English sections at Berkeley and one at Alameda Community College during my last year in graduate school. Then, in September of 1977, I began a two-year stint as a Freshman English instructor at the University of Santa Clara, where I had studied as an undergraduate ten years before. I returned to Berkeley for two summers, to teach Subject A (Berkeley's basic writing course for incoming freshmen) and then, for the School of Education, a special writing course for graduate students working on their theses. I left California in the summer of 1979 for a permanent teaching position in the English department here at Radford, where, except for one year of sabbatical leave, I have taught ever since.

Today Young 405 becomes all the classrooms in which I have ever taught. I imagine Colleen sitting among years of students I have known. Torrie Cox is in the second row near the door. The first time I call on her in class, she says, "Sir!" startling me with her military courtesy. Craig Getzloff is in the back of the fourth row, looking down at his notes. Suddenly his head shoots up and he smiles to discover me writing one of his sentences on the chalkboard. I put it up anonymously to illustrate illogical coordination. Craig's first smile means he does not mind. He studies the sentence. His second smile acknowledges the glitch he finds in his own words.

One student—I don't remember her name; I have forgotten many of their names; I will call her Lisa—sat in the front of the room. The day we talked in class about Robert Hayden's "Those Winter Sundays," Lisa didn't raise her hand, didn't speak, looked pale, even sick. But later she told me that the poem made her see something about her own father that she had never considered before. The cold, the stove, the polished shoes, the angers that shook the house—these were from *her*

15

house, she said. This was *her* father. This was the tangled sadness and affection of her own childhood. She was silenced by
memory.

After one class at the University of Santa Clara, Gerhard
Behrans, Tom Kovacs, and Paul Ganz paused in the hall. We
had been talking about E. B. White's essay "Once More to the
Lake." I had brought up the last line: ". . . my groin felt the chill
of death." The students balked, looked quizzical and disappointed. Up to that point, they understood pretty much what
White was getting at, remembering his summers as a boy in
Maine, reliving them now with his young son. They could see
what he meant about the cabins and the camp store and the
moonlight cruises dreaming of girls and the afternoon thunderstorms. But the wet swimming trunks and the chill of death?

"Well, we hope the next essay is better than this one,"
Gerhard said to me after class in the corridor.

"Wait a minute," I said to the three of them. I tried again:
"The chill the boy feels is just the shock of those cold swimming
trunks he's trying to pull on, but his father's growing old. He
feels death, in his groin, in the passing of his sexual life."

They looked at me and started to smile. Everywhere around
us in Kenna Hall were girls in shorts and tank tops, arms bare
in the northern California spring, long hair. Gerhard had been
out on the reservoir in Los Gatos that morning at 5:30 rowing
with the varsity crew, his feet strapped to the stretcher board,
his hands feathering the oar at the end of each pull through the
water, four fifteen-hundred-meter sprints before the sun was up.
Now it was 11:00. In an hour the three of them would be meeting friends for lunch across the street at Benson. And before
the words were out of Tom's mouth, I knew what they were
thinking.

"*Oh*," he said with a dramatic inflection, drawing it out facetiously, "well, sure. If you're getting old. But . . ." I did not
even wait for him to finish. I just laughed, pleased to be standing there with them, laughing together, sharing our own version
of White's double vision. "Get out of here, you guys," I said.

When I left Moreau High School, I was dispirited by what I
took to be the immaturity of my students, by my own ignorance, by the drain of the schedule and the sheer labor of the

work. Yet for all the years I was in graduate school, Chris Davis came by regularly to see me, for talk and lunch on the stone benches of Sproul Plaza until I'd have to leave for class or the carrel room in Wheeler where I was working on my dissertation. During that time, he finished high school, finished college, earned his teaching credential, and began his own career as a high school English teacher. It was the playing out of what his father had said years earlier to me in a parent-teacher conference when Chris was in the tenth grade. For ten minutes or so, we talked generally about the class, recent assignments, the boy's satisfactory progress. Then, as they were getting up to leave, his father said what he had come to say: thanks for helping Chris so, for making him want to do his work and feel good about it.

Mary Beth Gannett is here in this classroom of memory, too. One day I read a draft of an essay aloud to her class. In it I told some stories from my own experience as a writer to illustrate how the sounds of sentences enchanted me. I asked the students for their reaction. The talk was animated. It pushed past the hour, and as students gathered their things to leave the room a small group gathered around at the front to continue the talk. Mary Beth stood at the edge of the group and waited to catch my eye. "Keep working on it," she mouthed across the shoulders of those in front; "keep going with it." Then she smiled and left.

I sent a draft of the same essay to one of my former students, Diane Bumpass, who became an insurance actuary after graduation. She wrote back to say that she too had heard that enchantment in my voice when I read aloud in class. She heard it when she took courses from me, and (she went on to disclose what I had never known) she heard it later, too. She looked up the schedule of my classes. Some afternoons she would study in the hall where I taught, doing calculus problems on the wooden bench against the cinder block walls. Some days she would stand outside the classroom door and listen for my voice reading, say, a poem by Hopkins: "my heart in hiding stirred for the bird / the achieve of, the mastery of the thing!"

I am grateful for images such as hers. Our relations to each other, teacher and student, are so complicated that images are sometimes more exact than analysis can ever be. Diane's letter from years later helps me understand at least part of my life as a teacher: I am in the closed classroom, she in the empty hall outside. Our hearts are in hiding.

On Tuesday, Colleen and her classmates will be remembering, too. Some of them will have had a teacher like Phyllis Levy, the poet, who told them in eleventh grade that they had musical minds. She insisted students call her Phyllis. Her earrings were the most fabulous concoctions—feathers, shells, old spoons hammered flat. I imagine that one day Colleen got up the nerve, in a gesture that was part daring, part wonder, part affection, to just reach out and touch them. Long after Earth Shoes had been forgotten by everyone else, Phyllis still wore hers, and every evening (she told her classes) she sat at her potter's wheel for at least an hour, her hands in wet red clay. Almost all of Phyllis's classes were devoted to writing something or other, and she would walk among the desks talking with students about what they were working on. Stroll, as if the room were a park, peeling an orange, looking over people's shoulders, every once in a while popping a wedge in her mouth.

Or perhaps they had someone like the twelfth-grade English teacher who told his students this: "I have written to the University of Georgia and Georgia Tech. I have talked to their faculties. These are the kinds of papers they require in Freshman Comp. These are the kinds of errors they take off points for. This is the correction sheet they use. That's why I call this 'College Composition.' We're going to do what they do, to get you ready. The reason I'm being such a stickler about all the formal details is that I want you to be prepared. When you've done this work in here, you'll know what they're asking you to do, and you'll be confident."

As I imagine their memories of teachers, it is my own remembering I project. That is part of how we know who we are in school (as elsewhere), remembering who and where we have been.

Terry Loughran said, "Think, Rich, think," when I was enrolled in his ninth-grade world history course at St. Joseph's Seminary High School in Mountain View. I still have the notebook he required us to keep, full of maps I made of ancient

Greece and drawings of Roman clothing and sketches of the battle movements of the Persian Wars. I think he had us building balsa catapults to complement our study of the sieges of the Crusades; but whatever it was, I can still see the water and steam pipes along the ceiling of the basement utility tunnel through which he and I were walking one afternoon to get to the workshop. Whatever it was, we were building it together, and it was for both of us, I could sense, that he wanted me to think.

The Freshman English course I took at St. John's College Seminary was nothing like any that I have taught since; it included no writing, just the reading and close analysis of essays. But the teacher of that course, Louis Franz, had a mesmerizing effect on me. His face gleamed. His cuff links gleamed. His eyes were narrow, his laugh hard. He expected us to memorize the particular structures of essays by writers like C. S. Lewis and John Henry Newman, and to show us what he meant he memorized them himself. I could not help admiring him, not only for the tour de force of his classroom presentations, but for the generosity of his work with us outside of class. It was he who introduced us to "The Waste Land" by arranging for us to listen one evening after dinner to Eliot's recorded reading of the poem. And the next year, when a group of us were studying British literature together, he shared with us a paper he had written on the nature of tragedy. It was the first time I had ever read anything one of my teachers wrote.

Ralph Rader not only shared finished papers he had written with us; he wrote *to* us, informally, single-spaced, the page jammed with his thought, all the erasures and corrections and second thoughts showing. That was at Berkeley in 1970, a course in the problems of literary scholarship. It was the single most challenging, clarifying, satisfying course I took as a graduate student, and it led, eventually, to my asking Rader to direct my dissertation. But the most compelling memory I have of him today is neither of his writing nor of our later work together. It is of his crowded red Chevrolet pulled up in front of my house in Oakland one spring evening. The term was over. I had written the final paper for his course. He had read and graded it. And since he was out for a drive with his family, he said when he came to the door—as if such things were a matter of course—he thought he would bring it by. I had never heard of such a thing; full professors did not hand deliver graduate student papers during family drives. As simple a gesture as it was, it seemed extraordinary to me, and it made me feel honored.

Looking at this empty room today, I recall particular moments from different years of teaching. One time when I taught at Moreau High School, the class was divided into groups to argue among themselves about a subject I've forgotten. Perhaps it was the question of what happened to Kurtz in the jungle of *Heart of Darkness*. Perhaps it was whether they believed police treated people fairly (we had been reading John Hersey's *Algiers Motel Incident*). The noise of their talk grew. The dean of students peered sharply through the tiny window in the door. His face made me feel suddenly guilty for the lesson I was teaching. Framed there for an instant in the glass, it aligned me suddenly with the students against his discipline.

In English 2, a freshman course I taught at the University of Santa Clara, we made a book of essays on the Great Depression, collected writing from everyone in class, illustrated the pieces, duplicated and bound the whole. For my contribution (the students wanted me to submit a piece of writing, too), I interviewed my father and merged some of his stories of a Northampton boyhood with those of Studs Terkel and Arthur Schlesinger. When the book was finished, we celebrated with a publication party: pepperoni pizza, tortilla chips, Oreos, and Coke. We read around in the freshly printed collection, admired each other's work, and picked up our litter. Some students asked each other to sign their books.

I remember visitors to my classes, too, my sister Eileen and my wife, Susie, and my mother- and father-in-law (after a discussion of "A Modest Proposal," they said kindly that they wished I had been one of their teachers). When I was a graduate student at Berkeley, the then director of Freshman English, Frederick Crews, visited my class one afternoon and admired the way I made it around to nearly all students for brief in-class conferences on their work in progress. As we walked away from Dwinelle, talking about what he'd observed, he noted sympathetically that it was surely nervousness that made me say

"OK?" after nearly every sentence. It was certainly nerves I felt the morning I looked up and saw a Radford graduate student I was supervising in *her* teaching sitting in the back of *my* class. "Oh, no," I thought, "now she'll see how it really is." And it was to a class on *Mrs. Dalloway* that my friend from graduate school Richard Rodriguez happened to come. Writing later about that class, he said that what he had seen was teaching with such desire that it was as if I were pushing my way out of the grave.

The students in Colleen's class on Tuesday will be hopeful and apprehensive. I will be, too. We will interview each other in pairs, then introduce one another to the larger group. Someone will ask me, "Do you have a family? children? Where did you come from?" It will be clear from my accent that I am not from southwestern Virginia. "How long have you been teaching here?" I will answer with animation and a smile, with all the energy and courtesy I can. For, however many times I have started over, this is it: we are new; this is our beginning. And whoever we are, wherever we come from, however fresh or worn, we are—in this time and this place—working together.

2

Lacrimae Rerum

> Can you come here as a kid and learn anything? It looks to
> me as though you could come here . . . and learn just
> about anything you wanted to learn. You could learn bas-
> ketball, soccer, the classics, Spanish, geography, comput-
> ers; how to play the oboe, learn to draw, paint, and use the
> potter's wheel; how to use the library; certainly learn to
> diagram sentences, take notes, write essays and book re-
> ports . . . we have this stuff, and we, the teachers, know
> about it and you can learn about all this and plenty else,
> right here. . . . So with all this stuff, these books, those
> films, basketballs, class lists, teachers, and so on, then why
> doesn't this school work?
>
> —James Herndon
> *Notes from a Schoolteacher*

JAMES HERNDON IS an iconoclastic junior high social studies
teacher from a school district he facetiously calls Tierra Firma.
His vision of American education is comic. He looks at schools
and the people in them with the keen wildness of Aristophanes,
Erasmus, or Swift. He draws portraits of students and parents
and teachers and principals and custodians and coaches that are
just outrageous enough to represent the energy and dedication,
laziness, ill will, and preposterous hope of all of us connected
with schools. As idiosyncratic as they are, the teachers and students at Spanish Main Junior High School are so familiar that
Herndon could be talking about all the schools I have taught at,
about their students and teachers, about me.

The winter in which Teresa Simpson took Freshman English from me, her work just seemed to get worse and worse. After writing that beautiful paper about her mother, she submitted a gray, sickly, flu-inspired research essay. Then she turned her mind to a biographical sketch of one of the authors she had read in the course anthology. We had studied *Antigone*, so Teresa chose Sophocles as her subject. The assignment should have been simple, one or two pages, two biographical sources. But it must have baffled her.

Based on the paper she ended up with, I imagine that the library was a maze to her. She had completed orientation exercises and taken the guided tour with the class. But as soon as she got over to McConnell on her own, she must have felt lost. The aisles seemed dark, the stacks towering. At the end of each row she saw a reflection of herself—a little girl wandering around, not knowing what she was doing. Somehow, she couldn't explain it, she found her way to some books with information on Sophocles, photocopied the pages, and wrote up the summary. Though the result must have looked strange to her, she was glad to be finished. She had what was called for and turned it in. Her first sentence declared that Sophocles was a "rich industrialist," the next that "he was one of the most picturesque figures in American education." The two sources she used were *The Oxford Classical Dictionary* and the *Dictionary of American Biography*, both of which she duly cited. Hers was an honestly befuddled paper. It told the story of a composite Sophocles, made up of fragments of the lives of two men born twenty-three hundred years apart, one who lived in Athens and one who lived in Massachusetts.

Perhaps I should have felt worse about this result than I did—about my not providing enough instruction for Teresa to do the assignment correctly; about her not recognizing or fixing the nonsense. But as usual she was buoyant. Even as her work grew less satisfactory, and her interest in the course waned, she seemed to become happier. The flu was past; the lawn on Muse Quad was greening. Whatever it was that was happening in Freshman English, her brightness kept reminding me that winter was in fact giving way to spring.

And when I was tempted to become too sober about her

failure, I had to admit that I recognized in her story something of my own. Libraries still disorient me; I more often stumble on what I need than find it by systematic search. As helpful as librarians are, and as necessary as I know their help is, I still must overcome a deep reluctance to ask for it. I have been lost in the same aisles that confused Teresa and submitted papers I wrote but did not understand.

The first semester I was a graduate student at Berkeley, I did a seminar paper on allegory in *Piers Plowman*. I can't now reconstruct either the assignment we were given or the substance of my essay. What I remember better are the sharpened pencils our young professor brought to class and laid on the seminar table next to his copy of the text. The morning light coming in through the high window behind him, shadowing his face. The astonishment I felt at Sproul Plaza as I made my way to class. (Even in the morning the plaza was alive: tables set up already soliciting petition signatures; small knots of men, young and old, arguing violently in languages I could not recognize; dogs and pigeons; blown sheets of newspaper; kiosks plastered with circulars for massage, poetry readings, Japanese films, political rallies; young women in sandals and flowered dresses drinking coffee on the wood benches and reading the *Daily Cal*: a field full of folk.) This was unlike anywhere I had ever gone to school. I stayed up late the night before the paper was due, finishing and typing it at the coffee table of my tiny apartment, sure all the while that I did not know what I was talking about, but hoping that somehow it would satisfy.

"Do you intend to get a Ph.D. here?" my professor asked in his soft voice the day he gave me back my paper. I nodded. "Then you'd better learn how to write."

I was flayed by those two sentences. They scraped across my mind like a wire brush. He might have helped me see where and how my writing was unsuccessful (I already knew it was) and suggested some ways of thinking about allegory or about analytical papers that would have been instructive to me. He had written comments on my pages, of course, in pencil, but after what he said, I could never manage to give them my full attention. Still, I think the cruelty of his remark was probably inadvertent. And if I remember the *Piers Plowman* paper when I recall Teresa's biographical sketch of Sophocles, I hear in that teacher's remark my own meanness.

Years later, in an introductory literature class, Liz complained aloud about *Paradise Lost*: "But I don't under*stand* this stuff. I can't *read* it." Suddenly I was impatient. I pictured her spending a few minutes on it, then giving up. I remembered the times she admitted not having done the assigned reading. I heard the whine in her voice. I said, to her and to the whole class, with a whine of my own, "Anyone whose native language is English can read this."

It was as if I had slapped her. She was mortified, she told me later, to be told in class that she not only couldn't make sense of *Paradise Lost* but didn't understand English. I wanted to explain what I had meant: that the syntax of the poem can give us clues to reading it, that tracing its sentences as sentences can help us through its baroque surface. I wanted to say that I didn't mean it as an insult, either to Liz or to any of the other students who felt confused and uncertain in reading the poem. Still, I remembered my impatience and knew that she was right.

Henry Adams says of his years as a student and teacher at Harvard that "the chief wonder of education is that it does not ruin everybody concerned in it, teachers and taught." Adams's wonder is the same as Herndon's, their formulations simply opposite angles on the same point: Why doesn't this school work? Why doesn't this school ruin us? I share their puzzled surprise, but I think one answer to both questions is that school is less a place than a relationship between persons. Weaknesses deeper than ignorance swamp the interaction between teachers and students; virtues greater than competence animate it. It's enough to make one alternately despair and rejoice.

I audited a lecture course in Milton one term. The window shades, pulled down against the afternoon sun, cast a yellow pall over the wood floor and the wooden desks scattered haphazardly through the room. It was always afternoon in that room, the slanting sun always warm. The lecturer spoke from notes in a manila folder. Sometimes he stopped to read a passage from his worn copy of the text. One day he lectured on the Latin exercises Milton was assigned as an undergraduate, one day on the hierarchy of poetic forms as they were understood in the Renaissance, one day on the genesis of English meter in the quantitative metrics of Greek. I had a pressing purpose in that course, preparing for my master's degree comprehensive examination. You'd think I would have been attending to every word. Yet I faded. The professor would be explaining, say, the physics of spirit by which the angels in *Paradise Lost* could be said to have bodies, and the amber shades and floor and desks would flow together into a warm bath of soft light. When I woke, I would find my notes dribbling off into a sagging line in mid-sentence.

Sometimes the interactions between teachers and students are more unsettling than falling asleep in lecture. My younger son's first-grade teacher told me that he was uncooperative. "Stephen cannot control himself," she said. "He misbehaves and disturbs the other children. He's not mean or malicious, just undisciplined." First grade. Stephen had been in school three months. He rolled the pencil off his desk. The teacher took away his chair and made him stand throughout the rest of the lesson. He rolled his pencil off the desk again. She asked the class to vote on whether Stephen should be made to stand in the hall (they voted that he should).

The principal concurred with the teacher's assessment: "Stephen needs to understand the rules of school. He's a little bit of a troublemaker, you know, and not just in class. In phys ed, in the cafeteria, in the halls. The boy needs to knuckle down, that's all. He thinks he's supposed to *like* school." The principal looked at me across his desk, took another swallow of coffee, and said with an expansive, confidential laugh: "Hell, Rich, *none* of us liked school."

One afternoon in the teachers' lounge at Moreau High School—I had never imagined the loud and nervous bravado with which teachers could crow to one another—two of my colleagues were regaling us with a tale. For some misdemeanor I never got clear, they had decided to discipline one of the boys unofficially. The hall was empty when they cornered him, grabbed him each with one handful of belt and a fistful of shirt, lifted him clear off the ground and smashed him back into the lockers. It was the synchronized rhythm of their move that pleased them both, that and the sound of the boy hitting the wall. Before they were finished with him, they checked to see that his head had not dented the lockers. Their laughter echoes for me still, forced and afraid.

I can hear the bitter laugh of a graduate student, too. "What a *joke!*" she said, when the midterm examinations were handed back in the Milton course. Her exam had been marked with an A, but she was spluttering with anger. At the end of her essay, the professor had written a brief note that the student considered perfunctory. At the beginning of each of her answers to the fifteen objective questions, he had written in red pen a capital letter. He had not marked them wrong; he had given her full credit for each; he had simply corrected them. "*Je*-sus," she said to me, "Marking my capitalization? And almost nothing about my essay? What *is* this? *High* school?" She slammed her exam down, took a breath, and then said again, "What a joke."

Herndon praises the folly of schools and in so doing instructs us in their irremediable failures. He tells stories about himself and his colleagues and students, about their befuddlement and hubris, and declares candidly, "None of us had the slightest idea what to do." He makes me laugh. But when I put his book down and look around me at failure—my own, my teachers', my students'—I am saddened. When I realize that even if I could imagine a utopia in which all the talent, resources, money, power, and time were available, I couldn't design a school that would work; when I stop to realize that, I am stunned by futility.

"Lacrimae rerum."

I was sitting with Wayne Shumaker in his office on the second floor of Wheeler Hall, years after I had taken his Milton course, passed my comprehensive examination, and gone on to start work on my dissertation. We were eating homemade cheese sandwiches out of brown paper bags, our feet up on the sill of his open window.

"Do you know that phrase?" he asked me.

I told him I didn't.

"It's from Virgil," he said with an enigmatic smile. "It means 'the tears of things.'"

The first time I visited his office, my first term at Berkeley, he did not hear me tap on the oak door, which he had propped open to indicate that he was holding office hours. I stuck my head in. Bookshelves ran the length of one wall in the large, spare, high-ceilinged room. Wayne was standing at the blackboard opposite the shelves, chalk in hand, reading what was written there and thinking. The neck button of his long-sleeved white shirt was open, his brown-striped tie loose. On the board before him were several lines of poetry in English and beside them a block of Japanese ideograms. Before I tapped again, this time on the inside of the door, he had reached up and drawn the lines of another Japanese sign.

"Mr. Shumaker," I said. "Excuse me."

Abruptly he turned, put down the chalk, asked how he could help, drew me in to sit down, and began to load and tamp his pipe. Our business was brief: he had been assigned as my adviser that year; I needed him to sign my course schedule. I thanked him and withdrew, before he had had time even to light his pipe. But as I was going out the door, I noticed that he set it down unlit in the pipe rack on the table and reached again for the chalk.

I left as quickly as I did because I was afraid of him. He was perfectly courteous, but I felt disoriented. All those books, for one thing—no one I had ever known had so many books—the manifestly functional order of everything in his office, and the Japanese poem. Then, too, I had never seen anyone study standing up. I marveled at the agility of his concentration. One minute he was so absorbed in thought that he could not hear me at his door, the next he greeted me as wholeheartedly as if he had been waiting for me to arrive.

In addition to the Milton course, I took a small Latin seminar that Wayne conducted, later served as one of his assistants, and began to drop by his office on occasion for talk or lunch. I never told him my reaction to our first meeting; it would have seemed too odd to say I had been afraid. But everything I subsequently learned about him fit with that first image. The Japanese poetry, for example. It was the differences, he said, that interested him so. Teaching in Japan, then later serving in the intelligence service there, he had been struck by the recognition that human beings could view life so differently. That's what

Wayne had been trying to stress about Milton, urging us to read him not as if he were *like* us, but as if he were different.

"Do you know Ruth Benedict's *Patterns of Culture?*" he asked me—in the way he always introduced me to things I did not know and thereby connected me at once to Milton, cultural anthropology, and a young Japanese deckhand he had once seen on a ship in the Pacific. The young man stood alone in the bow, leaning into the wind, singing a song that Wayne could not understand. I can't remember now whether, like Wordsworth, he said he didn't understand because the words were strange or because the wind obscured them. Whatever the reason, the image of that singer remained with him precisely because he could not comprehend it, because it figured for him indelibly the mystery of life.

The young sailor's body leaning against the wind reminds me of Wayne's, as quick and light as on the first afternoon we met. Like the prose of his sentences, it is both graceful and unassuming. Most days he walked to work; many afternoons he took time out for a swim. He sat in a hard wooden chair at his desk, stood at the blackboard or at the easel in his basement painting watercolors. Some of my most vivid memories picture him in motion: leading me out to admire the steps he had designed and built by hand in his backyard; jumping up from the chair in his office to grab a book to loan to me; reaching down to lift and hug my four-year-old son, Kevin.

It was the first time Wayne came to our house. He was hardly inside the front door before he had squatted down to greet Kevin. In a moment my son was in his arms. When I remarked on this greeting, Wayne laughed and shrugged, explaining that he was a grandfather. Then he told me a story about his own life as a scholar and a father. He had used to bring his work home, to continue it in a room he had fitted out for himself as a study. One evening, after some period of concentrated work, he found his young son curled up on the floor on the other side of the door where he had fallen asleep waiting. Wayne was struck with remorse, he told me, and decided from then on never to bring work home, for fear that he would prefer it to his children.

"Life is more complicated than it seems," Wayne would say

during our lunches in those years next to the open window, overlooking Strawberry Creek. About Milton's theology, about witchcraft, about watercolors, about engineering, about fatherhood—he would tamp his pipe, and smile his enigmatic smile, and say that all these things are more complicated than they seem.

I could not have predicted how much I would learn from him the day I first visited his office. I dozed in the warm amber light of his classroom. But one afternoon he startled me. He was lecturing on "Lycidas," Milton's elegy for his friend Edward King drowned in 1637 on the Irish Sea. I went to my shelf recently, now more than twenty years later, to look again at the lines of the poem that Wayne began to read:

> For *Lycidas* is dead, dead ere his prime,
> Young *Lycidas*, and hath not left his peer:
> Who would not sing for *Lycidas*? he knew
> Himself to sing, and build the lofty rhyme.
> He must not float upon his wat'ry bier
> Unwept, and welter to the parching wind,
> Without the meed of some melodious tear.

Wayne's voice read modestly, as usual. Then he paused, and after a moment he said, "I'll just stop there. I'm afraid that if I read more I will begin to weep."

I think I was still looking down at my own book when he spoke, still waiting to follow along as he recited. I looked up, amazed at his words, unsure that I had heard correctly. There he was as usual, the herringbone sport coat, buttoned, white shirt, tie, the lectern, the notes, the text. I don't know what he went on to say that afternoon in the rest of his lecture. Everything about the course has come to center for me in that one sentence about "Lycidas." It seemed to me then, and it seems to me today, an extraordinary, an extravagant, gift.

As it happened, we both came to the end of our time at Berkeley the same year, he to retire, me to graduate. During one lunch that last spring, he said, "Oh, how I envy you. You have so much to look forward to." When I came to Radford University, I wrote to thank him for everything, particularly for that moment in the lecture on "Lycidas." I wrote to say that I was trying to let his example inform my own teaching. Wayne replied with his customary courtesy that he was sure I would find my own way.

In searching for that way, I have encountered more waste and sadness than I ever imagined. Teaching, like everything else, partakes of the *lacrimae rerum*. But I have also discovered that even the puzzle of school is more complicated than it seems. When I remember what seemed in my callow ignorance like the remoteness of Wayne's lectures, when I feel again the dusky amber light of his classroom and the fresh welcome of his office, when I let my memory linger on our bag lunches and easy talks together about everything under the sun, I discover that I am deeply glad.

3

His Son the Writing Teacher

TWO SUMMERS BEFORE my father died in 1989, he came to stay with us on Vashon, an island in Puget Sound in northwest Washington. He brought sixteen pages of writing about his childhood and youth in Massachusetts and about his early adventures on the road. He nonchalantly gave them to me, then sat across the room by the window and watched me read. He held his breath. I told him they were wonderful, that I loved reading them, was glad he had brought them to share with me.

In the last years of his life, we would talk nearly every Sunday night on the phone, he sitting in the recliner in the den in Oakland, I leaning against the doorjamb of the breakfast room in Radford.

"We should write a book," he said, joking.

"You should write these stories down," I said.

He brought the first pages with him for me to read. They were full of episodes I had never heard. Of the time he carried a squirrel he had caught into the kitchen to show his grandmother Towhill and let it get away to race around the room, eluding the family dog and terrifying the old woman. Of the wake of his grandfather, for which the front parlor window, casing and all, had to be removed in order to get the casket into and out of the house. Of the evening they all heard an explosion and ran upstairs to find his father smiling, shotgun in hand at the window, having picked a pheasant off the fence. Of the weekly subscription to *Argosy* that his stepmother, Annie, would read to the assembled family on Saturday night, she sitting in the center of the kitchen floor on a stool. Of the feelings of anger and scorn that he was daily subjected to, living with his father, the only child in the home of his proud stepmother's parents.

From one memory to the next, his past blossomed and flourished, the layers of one story peeling open to reveal another and another. He had only gotten as far as New Orleans in his chronicle, up to when he was about twenty, and already he realized the enormity of his task. Fifty years to go, and he hadn't even begun to exhaust the early years yet.

Like the distribution of his grandfather's estate. Had he told me about that? I said no, I didn't think so, and realized that it was hard for him to tell what he had actually written and what he had said or merely thought.

"Oh, there are so many stories," he said.

Norma, my stepmother, had warned me over the phone before they came: "He's lost a lot of weight since you saw him last. The Amiodarone has thinned the skin of his face. Sometimes he looks pretty blue." Even warned, I didn't recognize him when he came off the plane.

Tell me about your life, I asked him; I can help you write it down.

Let me tell you about my life, he said; you're my son the writing teacher.

The years Susie and I have known one another contain vastly more than those moments in which we think of ourselves as linked together by writing. Yet, so important do they now seem, it is impossible for me to imagine what our life, what we, would have been without them.

The spring of our last year at the University of Santa Clara, we lay as many afternoons as possible in the rose garden sun, feeling guilty only because Susie had work still to do on her senior thesis in philosophy. At the end of that term, she sat up after midnight drinking coffee in a San Jose pancake house listening to me read the final paper for my theology seminar. (We didn't call it a draft; neither of us knew anything about drafts in those days; a paper was written, then typed.) I drove down to Fresno during our first year of graduate school for one long weekend at the kitchen table of her apartment, both of us writing papers, one on *The Children of Sanchez*, one on *Bleak House*; both were lousy, but at least they were done. When our children reached preschool age, Susie worked with each of them to make books for me for Christmas, bringing her skills as an elementary school teacher home to our family. She typed up the children's dictated stories, sewed the sheets into signatures, cut the cardboard covers, helped the children glue on the fabric and paste in the pages, and transcribed a brief note "About the Author" to go on the last page under a photograph: "Christine Murphy is eight years old. This is her fifth book. She is giving it to her father. Christine's birthday is the day before Halloween. She gives a book to her father every year. She has designed lots of books. She lives in Radford, Virginia."

When the annual conference of the American Educational Research Association was held in Washington, D.C., in 1987, I spent the meeting in our hotel room, the chapters of Susie's dissertation draft spread out on the bed, reading and commenting on them. Between conference sessions, she would rush back to the room to check how far I had gotten and what I thought. When the first drafts of the chapters of this book were written in the spring of 1989, she spread them out on the floor of our living room and sat with me there, looking at them and helping me think about their scope and sequence.

In the course of my job as a writing teacher, I've learned many things about writing that neither Susie nor I knew twenty-five years ago when we first read our school papers to one another. In reading the literature of the profession, talking with colleagues, working with students, I have learned about free-writing, revision, and audience; about the sometimes vexed processes by which our ideas are confused and clarified in writing; about the rhetorical assets and liabilities of permitting academic writing to be personal. I have brought those things home (as Susie brought home the techniques for making children's books). They are part of our conversation, part of our life.

"I know it's late," she says, "but before you go to bed, could you help me edit this column I'm writing for the *Journal of Reading*? I need to cut about three hundred words."

Or I come up to the bedroom after a night class and find her reading a draft of an essay I'm thinking of sending to *English Education*. I've asked for her reaction, especially because she spends so much of her professional life now educating new teachers. She's in a flannel nightgown with blue flowers and a lace yoke. She has her glasses on and a black felt-tipped pen in her hand, and she turns the pages slowly. I slip into bed quietly, pick something off the nightstand to read while I wait, and pretend that I'm not holding my breath, anxious for her to finish.

The week my father came to visit, we talked again and again about his writing and his memories. Even on our garbage run, he was rehearsing stories he might tell. We squashed five thirty-gallon cans into the back of the station wagon, then drove up Robinson Point Road, over to Portage, past Tramp Harbor, up to Center and onto the dump road. All the way, our arms hanging out the open windows, we talked.

"I've told you about the gun, haven't I?" he asked after one pause.

The barrel was black enamel, the stock a walnut that glistened. He had seen pictures of Daisy BB rifles in the *Argosy* and had wanted one so badly that he had not even told anyone about it. His desire was fantastic. He knew that in his grandmother's house no boy would ever have a gun.

But, wondrously, his father had given him one for Christmas. He sat with it for hours in his lap, running his hands over the barrel, the trigger, the stock, the cocking lever, feeling their grain and texture in his fingers. He carried it unloaded into the field behind his house and pretended to shoot the stump of their old ash tree and a rotten pumpkin half covered with snow. His father brought home some target paper and fastened it to the back of the barn, and the two of them took turns aiming and shooting at the rings.

Before each shot, the Daisy needed to be cocked. My father was too small and weak to extend the lever simply with the fingers of his right hand, the way it was designed to be done. He watched his father cock the gun with ease, but when he was alone he worked out a method of his own. He would brace the butt of the stock on the ground between his feet, hold the barrel steady with his left hand, and reach down with his right to pull the cocking lever all the way up until it clicked. Then, as he lifted the gun to his shoulder, he would fold the lever back into place, shoot, and set the gun back down to cock again.

Once, just a few days after Christmas, when he tried to do this on the driveway back to the barn, he was standing by chance on a small patch of ice. As he pulled up on the spring-retarded lever, the stock somehow slipped away from his feet and the barrel jumped up into his mouth. The muzzle caught his lower teeth, smashing the two in the center.

"I've told you that story before, haven't I?" he said, turning toward me in the front seat of the station wagon, pointing to the gap in his lower teeth.

"Yes," I said. "But you didn't write about it."

"No." He paused. "I didn't want to. I didn't think it would be right. There was more to it than I've told you."

When I began teaching writing, I imagined that the job amounted to helping students increase their proficiency in the use of topic sentences, in structuring paragraphs, in keeping their subjects and verbs, pronouns and antecedents in agreement. Quickly it grew to more than that. Among many other things, I learned that I needed to try to help students conceive of the subjects they wrote about in ways that were important to them. I needed to help them discover that writing could foster their developing thinking, not just report thoughts already clearly defined. I learned that students needed help reflecting on themselves as writers and viewing the process of writing as essentially creative. But even as the job was growing more complex in my classroom and office, something entirely unexpected happened: I was bringing it home, and writing was coming to be one of the grounds on which my relationships with different members of my family were built. It was one of the ways we came to know one another, one of the ways we gave ourselves to each other.

When I passed the dissertation prospectus examination in 1974, I made a copy for my son Kevin—"Poetic Justice: A Study of the Critical Doctrine in the Early Eighteenth Century." He was five. At eighteen, he packed up his belongings to move out of our house in Radford and back to California. Among the things he took with him was my fourteen-year-old prospectus, still pressed between the covers of an inexpensive blue folder. When he was in the fourth grade, his teacher assigned a term paper on one of the California missions. He picked Santa Clara (because I was teaching at the university there), and the two of us drove down to talk to the archivist, to look at displays of early pictures and historical artifacts, and to explore the site where the mission had originally been built. He was proud of the paper that resulted, about Father Frey Tomas de la Pena and the Costanoan Indians. And he was proud to let me use it in in-service workshops with teachers to illustrate how one source of clarity in a thesis may be the writer's personal investment in the subject.

Rarely did our daughter, Christine, ask either Susie or me for help with her writing. She developed a coherent and detailed conception of what a "paper" is, and she acquired over the years in school and from her own extensive reading a considerable repertoire of writing strategies. After a brief orientation, and with only a few commands written down on an orange file card, she taught herself to use WordPerfect on our home computer. Though, as she tells me now, her friends and teachers regularly advised her to get help from us, she rarely thought she needed to. Instead, she would turn to me from the keyboard and ask, ad hoc, out of the blue: "What's another way to say, 'They held power in the place'?" or "How do you footnote a museum brochure?"

Only once can I remember her asking for my feedback on a draft of her writing. Before she typed up the essays for her college applications, she showed them to me. One was about her career goals. It began:

> Since I was about eight years old, I have wanted to be a school teacher. What first attracted me to this particular profession was not my love of children or even my desire to cultivate young minds. It was the way that Mrs. Woods, my third grade teacher, held the chalk when she wrote on the board. She would grasp the chalk (always a long, fresh, new piece) firmly in her hand and write very distinctly on the board about Columbus and long division, and anything else that was relevant to a third grade class in 1982. I wanted to be just like Mrs. Woods.

Christine wanted to know if her essay was, as she put it, too "cheesy." I said I didn't think so and complimented her on the freshness and particularity of her opening. Then I marveled to myself at what she wrote about us—something she had never said *to* us—her teacher-parents:

> Although they rush to meet deadlines, and they complain about obnoxious students, they really do love their jobs. They enjoy teaching, and they revel in the joy that students feel when they succeed. . . . A teacher must be dedicated, dedicated enough to spend his weekend baking muffins for an eight o'clock class on Monday morning. A teacher must be caring, so caring that she will spend all night on the telephone with a distraught student. Teachers must be hardworking. . . . A teacher must have all of these qualities, and many more. These are the qualities that I have seen when I have watched my parents.

I felt like an eavesdropper. Only later did it occur to me that perhaps, even here, she didn't want my advice. Perhaps she realized that she had never told us of her admiration, and this was her chance. At any rate, her first Thanksgiving back from college, she brought home the paper she'd recently been working on in Freshman English. She wasn't asking for my help thinking about writing it. What she wanted was my opinion of her teacher's comments on it and his grade. We brought all the drafts she'd written and the comments she'd received down to the Laundromat, loaded up the family wash along with hers from school, sat on a bench together amid the lint, and read.

Nearly every year now, in spite of some good-natured grumbling, Susie and I and our children gather to write what we call the family journal, a joint recollection of the events of the preceding year. Everyone talks while someone (usually I) transcribes what is said. Anything goes: whatever anyone remembers, I put down. The drive across the United States from Radford to Vashon Island, five people and a dog. Christine's being selected as a varsity cheerleader, Stephen's dropping the cake he and I made and frosted for the Cub Scout meeting, Susie's finishing her doctorate, my breaking my foot in a pick-up game of basketball, Kevin's being accepted at UCLA. Sometimes our memories build coherently on each other's. Sometimes the conversation—it's not a conversation exactly, more a joint composition—veers away to a totally new subject. No matter. I record it. If the talk flags, I say, "I'm waiting. . . . What else do you remember?" Always someone thinks of something more to include.

"No," Kevin finally said the last time, when Stephen was about to fill another pause. "Don't say it. Don't say *anything*. The only way to get him to stop writing is for all of us to be absolutely silent, absolutely still. If we say anything, he'll keep writing."

After my father died I found the pages he had brought with him to Vashon. They were in his desk drawer along with preliminary handwritten notes to himself for things to include in his life story. First, he sketched out the material, then expanded it as he typed. He was new to computers:

> This is the third time that I have tried to use this instrument, I have remembered to put this material on Dick's Disk, hopefully . . . I can save these thoughts from extinction. The first time I used this machine I forgot to save the material and lost all that I had written. The second time I attacked the machine and was moving along in fine fashion until I was interrupted by a phone call. As I returned to the machine I discovered that the screen was blank because of a power outage. . . . Actually this machine scares me to death. I not only have to remember how to operate it but I have to think of what I am going to say.

Though the computer may have unnerved him, he was fascinated by the stories. All his life he would tell them, his own and others', at the dinner table, over drinks, in his car with real estate clients on their way to look at a house. He was a wonderful salesman for the same reason that he was a wonderful storyteller: he could empathize with others, feel in his own bones their marrow. As much as he admired me for what I did well, it was that which he most hoped I could learn to acquire, a sympathetic imagination.

He took me to see Rita Tushingham in *A Taste of Honey*. The Northside Theater on Euclid Street in Berkeley was small, beat-up, just the sort of movie house in which to see a film about people down on their luck, themselves beaten up but somehow making do. Their resiliency cheered my father. His voice recounting their story for me as we walked back to the car was full of happiness. In the middle of *Hope and Glory* years later, when the characters surrounded by rubble from the London blitz suddenly begin to sing "The White Cliffs of Dover," my father, sitting next to me in the dark theater, couldn't contain himself. He joined in, first humming, then singing the words softly, aloud: "There'll be love and laughter and tears ever after . . ." Another time, we went together to see *Midnight Cowboy*. In his silence afterward, I reran the images of two grizzled men trying to survive winter in an abandoned New York tenement, of their trying to get to warmer weather before Rizzo would die, of the look on Joe Buck's face as the bus carried him and his dead friend, too late, into Miami. I thought my father had disliked the film. It was a long time before he spoke. "That could have been my story, Rich," he finally said, with more weariness than I had ever heard in his words.

The notes I found in his drawer indicate some of what he meant:

Hoboes on freight train south. Arrive Brownsville (broke). Went to Harlingen, Texas, to work at grapefruit juice plant 30 cents per hour. No overtime pay. . . . I hitchhiked to San Antonio and then to Del Rio on the Rio Grande. Slept in station of little town of "Judge Bean." Almost arrested by Texas Ranger. Riding flat car from El Paso to L.A. Had to say I was from L.A. to get across border. Freight to S.F. by way of Oakland. . . . Couldn't go to Alaska to canneries. Had to be union to be hired. Couldn't get in union. Lived 3rd and Mission. Cot—25 cents a night. Went broke. . . . I got a job between 5th and 6th and Market Streets [at a carnival arcade]. Three balls for a dime—shooting gallery— tattoo shop—army navy recruits hang out. My so called friend robbed me of what little money I had, took my clothes and left.

Most of the stories nested in these phrases were never told. The ones I did hear, abbreviated as they were, and recounted with his lilting animation and laughter, all contributed to the feeling I developed growing up that this life was a lark for him, the heady adventure of a reckless and lighthearted youth. Only later did I realize that he was on the road because his parents had grown hopelessly estranged from one another and home was no longer bearable for him. Only the night driving away from *Midnight Cowboy* did I begin to realize how frightened and desperate a boy he must have been.

"Hopefully I can save these thoughts from extinction," he wrote. As I read the first pages of his account of his life, he sat in the chair across the room and waited, watching me.

I tell stories about my family when I teach. They help to answer the questions students often ask the first day: Who are you? Where are you from? How did you end up here? They also help animate the reading and writing assignments I give students in my courses. This is reading and writing I value, the stories say; these issues are in the fabric of my life. Perhaps you will find some of their threads in yours as well.

I learned this anecdotal approach to teaching from Susie. For many years, she taught kindergarten. She told the children about her life away from school, about her husband and her children. When I visited her classroom, eyes would widen with wonder at the real person about whom the children had heard so much. Now, when I arrive to give a presentation on writing across the curriculum to her college language arts courses for prospective teachers, the students laugh and say, "So, *you're* Rich."

If it was Susie from whom I learned to tell personal stories in my classroom, I think it was from me that she learned to incorporate such material in her writing. For a critical essay on the artistry of Ouida Sebestyen's novels, she drew on her own experience and memory to explain some particularly vivid details. Salty Yeager, one of Sebestyen's characters, felt his way along a counter, hid his underwear in a box of Epsom salts, walked two dusty slippers up a wall. Susie's explanation of the effect on her of these moments is that "there were no Epsom salts in my grandmother's bathroom though there was a musty closet . . . Salty's story and mine are both made up of such secret corners."

After a winter in North Yorkshire when we enrolled our two younger children in the local comprehensive school, the editors of the *Virginia English Bulletin* asked Susie to submit an article comparing the schools in the north of England with those in the United States. She framed it with an account of an afternoon walk along a footpath in the Yorkshire dales: "Here I was, close to the end of my three-and-a-half-mile stroll (the map showed that I had only three more fields to cut across before I reached the parking lot and the short-cut back to our flat), out of breath, with the light fading in the onset of early dusk, and lost." What she had observed in the ways children were encouraged to learn in British schools was very similar to what she experienced finding her way with the help of a guidebook along those beautiful stone walls. Our children's British teachers, she wrote, "seemed to believe that figuring out what to learn and how to learn it was an important part of the learning process." In a similar way, she finally found the stile she was looking for. "The footpaths are complex," she concluded. "There are books that provide some suggestions, but even with their help walkers have to find their own way."

The year she first introduced the writing of family stories to students in her course in the teaching of reading, something happened that surprised her. She read some stories to the students, described some ways in which writing their own could enhance their understanding of the reading, and gave them time in class to sketch the beginnings of a story they could develop later. She wrote in class while they did, to model for them the activity, and suddenly, unexpectedly, she found herself pulled into her own narrative of childhood. The force of the assignment startled her.

When she was a young girl, before her family had moved to Vashon permanently to live, they spent as many weekends as possible on the island. Friday evenings, they would load up the station wagon—kids, clothes, pets, food, equipment, and whatever else would fit—and drive down to wait on the Fauntleroy dock for a ferry to take them across. The pets one time included a parakeet, an Irish terrier mutt, and a lamb; the food included a lemon meringue pie a friend had sent along for the family. As she wrote, Susie found herself remembering the moment. It was one her family had told over and over to themselves. Startled by something, the dog had begun to howl and set the bird to screeching. The lamb—frightened by all the commotion—had jumped over the back seat into the pie, and this had set the kids to crying in their turn. What made the memory so compelling for her, though, was that she felt it concentrate all her childhood—the rain-pooled dock, the thick night out of which ferry lights would eventually appear, her grandparents' little house in which they would stay, sleeping in a bedroom at the edge of a pebbly shore.

Sketching that memory had been a class activity for Susie, but unexpectedly she found herself doing what she had encouraged the students to do: working on it some more, turning her first notes into a story, trying to define her feeling more fully. When she finished, she read it to her class and then, printing it up like the books she helped our children make, gave it to her parents for Christmas. It was a family story after all, but it had become more, a way to thank them for the gift of those Friday evenings full of promise.

Susie's experience with that assignment surprised me, too. For some time I had been telling myself and her and other teachers and students in my classes that writing can enable us to feel and think, remember and understand. What I had forgotten (I forget it still) is that even the assignments I know are powerful can affect people more deeply than I anticipate. Even those benefits of writing I think I understand can be more complicated than they seem.

My father did not complete the chronicle of his life. We did not write the book he joked about. But he did finish telling me the story of the gun, even if he never finally wrote it down.

At the dump, I grunted the plastic cans out of the back of the station wagon, took off their lids, and tipped them over onto the soft dirt. My father collected and stacked the empty cans and lids, and we headed back to the house to wash them clean with the hose.

The dark gray winter afternoon went red. The boy held himself still on the ground. His hands pressed against his mouth, waiting for the ringing in his head to stop. It was some time before he tried to swallow, but when he finally did, he discovered his mouth full of warm soup and bits of rock. The pain in his jaw was still so sharp that when he tried to spit some of it out, he was unable to open his mouth or move his tongue, so the mixture dribbled through his lips and fingers and dripped brown onto the snow.

My father did not say how long he lay there, whether any light remained in the sky when he made his way back into the house. He left me to imagine with what fierce care his grandmother ascertained what had happened, how she cleaned his mouth, picked out the pieces of tooth, stanched the bleeding of his gums. I do not know how his father was told.

What kept it from being written, the part that kept it from being told until the day we drove home from the dump is this. That when the boy's father found out, he yanked him from the kitchen chair by the coat sleeve and dragged him into the yard to find the gun. The boy could not remember where it was. Since the light had already fallen, they searched along the icy driveway with their feet, the boy being dragged as his father's boots kicked and scuffed frantically. At last his father found it, up by the maple tree, and at last he let the boy go. He reached down into the snow, grabbed the Daisy by the barrel, and swung it with both hands at the trunk of the tree. Again and again he swung the rifle until it cracked, until the stock split and broke away from the metal, the firing mechanism popping open, its pins and springs ricocheting off the tree. The boy could not see his gun come apart, but he could hear it. All he could see was the shadowy form of his father flailing at the tree in the dark.

We drove in silence for a while.

"I think you should try to write that story," I finally said, leaning on the steering wheel and staring out, unseeing, at Puget Sound. "There's something in it that helps explain the loneliness of your childhood in that house. Something of the rage in the middle of which you grew up. Imagine what it must have cost him," I said, "to get that rifle for you. Imagine what he must have thought he was doing as Christmas approached and his gift to you grew secretly for him in his heart."

It was what I thought my father wanted to hear when he gave me his writing. I thought he was telling me those things because I was a writing teacher.

"I don't want to put that in," he said. "I don't feel it would

44

be right. It wouldn't be fair to him. To tell about him like that. It would give the wrong impression."

"But you don't have to be fair," I said. "And, anyway, what is fair? You're not trying to tell his story. You're trying to tell your own."

He was trying to do more than that. When we were finished spraying out the cans back at the house, my father looked up at me, a dripping lid in each hand.

"You know," he said, "I've been telling you what I think about my father."

The stress on "my" was very slight. The late-afternoon north wind blew the sky clean. It brought the snow-lined crests of the Cascades into focus and whipped the sound with froth.

"Sometime," he said, then paused, "sometime I'd like to ask you what you think about yours."

4

Learning to Teach

I HAD JUST turned twenty-three when I began teaching at Moreau High School in Hayward, California. Susie and I had married in June, and I had spent the summer working at a box factory down in the Port of Oakland. I was freckle-faced, five-eight, 135 pounds, Catholic. I wore a tie, but I looked like one of the students.

My old teachers and new colleagues gave me the same advice: don't smile. It's easier to start out strict, they said, and ease up on the kids as you go along, than it is to begin nice and later try to tighten up your control. The caution sounded so sensible that I grabbed it and, assuming the sternest face I could, began my teaching career.

I walked into my first classroom—thirty-five tenth-grade boys—with a lesson plan and a textbook, a class roll and a detention pad. I had never taught any sort of school before. I had taken no education course, held no teaching credential, had never seen an overhead projector. The teacher's desk was a raised wooden platform with a precarious high stool. I decided against trying to climb up onto it, but that left me standing, hardly able to see over the boys' heads.

Not smiling meant not smiling. It meant being all business and telling the class what I thought my purposes and objectives were. This is the sort of thing I said: "My name is Mr. Murphy. I will be your English teacher this year. I'm sure that all of you will have gotten the textbook on book day. This year we will read a number of the essays and stories in it. I will ask you to analyze those readings—to outline and paraphrase the essays, to summarize and interpret the stories. I will show you how to do these things, and I will ask you to write paragraphs and essays of your own."

Stiff—even I could hear it: "will have gotten"—but it sounded like what I remembered my own teachers saying and doing, so I felt I was on reasonably safe ground. Since the students were all quiet and watching me attentively, I imagined my presentation had the proper air of seriousness about it. When I said I hoped they would find the work enjoyable and personally rewarding, my mind felt a little jerk of something, as if I had caught my coat pocket on the corner of the desk. I did not quite believe my words, but I was not exactly lying either. So I pushed on, introducing myself and English 10.

Twenty years later, when I meet a new group of graduate students at Radford University ready to begin teaching Freshman English, I have lots of advice for them. I tell them to smile. I tell them to believe in the power and desire of students to learn. I tell them to be professional, to do their jobs seriously, to teach with joy, to share their writing with students, to invite students to work together as a community of learners, reading, responding to, and appreciating each other's work. I think it is sound advice, but I am not sure what good it does.

Many of these about-to-be-new-teachers have just earned their B.A.'s. Some look the age of their students, as if they might be sorority sisters or members of the same intramural basketball team. Most have never taught anything before. During a two-week workshop in August before they start teaching, they listen to veteran teachers. They read Peter Elbow and Donald Murray and write stories and talk together over cantaloupe slices and muffins and tea. They teach each other sample lessons and exchange class plans. Then, when the fall semester begins, they go into their classrooms alone.

If I knew what it was, I would tell you what they say to the new freshmen sitting in rows in front of them. But they are on their own. They come back exhilarated, flushed with the thrill of being in front of a class, full of stories to tell. They were so nervous, they say, that their hands and voices shook. They stood in the hall until the very last moment as the room filled, trying to look calm. They began class, panicked, excused themselves, went across the hall to the bathroom, stared for a moment into the mirror over the sink, and then walked back in and started over. Always they are amazed at the experience of asking students to interview one another and introduce each other to the class—and having the students actually *do* it. When, after a week or two, they receive their first set of student essays, they are astonished. They can hardly wait to read them; they carry the papers home in a new briefcase that finally has a purpose.

Their wonder and excitement are complicated by the same kind of fear I felt at the beginning. All the while they talk to their classes and take roll and describe assignments and answer questions, they are trying to remember what their teachers said and did, how they sounded. They are trying to fit themselves to a vague template in their minds. I think this is the single most important fact about the experience of new teachers, but it is not reserved for them. Many days even teachers who have been at this for a while feel what was impressed on us every day we were new: we are merely impersonating a teacher.

On the second day of my teaching career, I called out Anthony Edward's name. A boy said, "Here." I went on to Griffin and Gumpertz and Mason and Nichols and then finally registered that the class was snickering. I stopped, looked over the top of my black, horn-rimmed glasses at the rows of boys in front of me, willed them back into order, and proceeded. More snickering. I do not know how long it took me to recognize that John Wilson's voice was saying "Here" to everyone's name, but I finally did and the advice of my teachers was no help.

OK, so I'm not smiling. Now what do I do?

This, or some variant, happens almost every day in classrooms everywhere. We do not know what to do when the actual situation of our classroom does not correspond to the expectations we bring with us to our work. Sometimes we react with creative resourcefulness; sometimes we try to force our preconceived notion on the present. The class hasn't read the assignment? Give them a pop quiz. John Wilson won't keep his mouth shut? Send him to the office. It is for the rote application of clichéd reactions that we teachers become the butt of jokes. In our helplessness we become mechanical and, as philosopher Henri Bergson observes, comic.

Unfortunately, institutional education in America seems to have been devised largely to illustrate Bergson. It is built on a paradox. The standards, expectations, bureaucracy, and traditions of school all depend on the individual teacher's intelligence and creativity, but they also deliberately limit the scope of those personal qualities. Teachers and students are human beings, idiosyncratic and, within limits, free, but idiosyncrasy is just what the system wants to diminish. The success of schools seems to depend on regularizing human action, on mechanizing it. Providing something like equal education for a vast population of students requires uniformity, and uniformity cannot be approached without turning teaching into an increasingly robotic act. The more regimented and controlled teaching can be made, the more certain it is that the purposes of the educational system will be achieved.

In *Inquiry into Meaning*, Anne Bussis and her colleagues at the Educational Testing Service in Princeton have traced this paradoxical view of teaching to an illusion about technology with which they say we are enchanted. We associate technology with efficiency, they claim; one of its positive connotations for us is progress. When faced with the clumsy, intractable problems of school, we long for a technological solution. We want to remove uncertainty from the classroom. One apparent way to do so is to regiment teacher action with highly detailed curriculum guides and with checklists of good classroom practices.

Such regimentation has sometimes been based on a misapplication of educational research to school policy. Take, for example, the research finding that students learn more when teachers make the lesson's objective explicit. According to educational researcher Lee Shulman, some policymakers have translated that finding into a requirement that teachers explicitly tell students at the beginning of every class the objective of that day's lesson. Teachers who do not do so are reported as failing to demonstrate one of the so-called competencies of good teaching. Such a requirement misconceives both research and teaching. In it, Shulman argues, "teaching is trivialized, its complexities ignored, and its demands diminished." The act of teaching in context is far more complicated than any list of effective behaviors putatively sanctioned by controlled empirical investigation.

My own felt experience of the puzzle of school inclines me to agree. Teaching is a personal act and therefore finally resistant to complete formulation.

I borrow this notion from Michael Polanyi, the philosopher of science for whom knowing itself is personal and always fundamentally tacit. One reason that we know, in Polanyi's phrase, "more than we can tell" is that we do not focus on our knowledge. Riding a bicycle or playing the piano, hammering a nail or feeling with a probe for a dropped earring under the bureau—all require that we focus on the end toward which we are acting. In the midst of performing such acts, our minds are aware of their elements, of their sequence and relation to one another, of the heft and texture of the tools in our hands. But that awareness is only what Polanyi calls "subsidiary." Our focal awareness is directed at the end toward which we are coordinating all the separate, intricate elements of the act.

Our knowledge is also tacit when we anticipate a conception we have not yet formulated explicitly. According to Polanyi, scientists commonly intimate the existence of a problem to be solved which they do not yet understand and of an available, significant, but as yet unknown solution. Writers often have a similar experience. They recognize dimly the promise of a meaning toward which they work. They are unable yet to articulate that meaning, but they must know it tacitly because when it is finally written, part of their satisfaction takes the form of re-cognition, that is, of knowing *again*.

Sometimes what we know requires imaginative integration of a whole group of particulars. Polanyi illustrates that phenomenon with a general account of visual perception, but one of his recurring examples is our simple everyday recognition of a human face. The parts of a face are so complexly interrelated that our seeing them as a *whole* is an act of integrating imagination that even we cannot explain. A related kind of knowing— Polanyi calls it "topographic"—remains inarticulate, too. It involves reading and interpreting maps of all kinds—models, diagrams, two-dimensional illustrations—and construing them by means of an essential but inexpressible insight.

Practicing teachers are familiar with all these kinds of tacit knowing. When we conduct a lesson, we coordinate the dynamic elements of the class—presenting specific instructions, fielding questions, following the winding thread of discussion—trying to integrate them all within the plan we hope to realize. Our working days are full of intimations that guide our practice—the sense that a course is going well or not, for example; the hunch that an assignment we have developed should be changed to fit better the needs of these specific students. Every time we diagnose or evaluate a student's writing, we integrate particulars in much the way Polanyi describes seeing a face, recognizing its complex multiple parts as constituents of some coherent whole. When we read or write a syllabus, we do so with the tacit awareness of unspecified relationships among texts, assignments, the dynamic texture of class meetings, and the calendar of the term.

Polanyi does not claim that there is no such thing as explicit knowledge, only that much of our knowing is made up of tacit acts of intimation, recognition, interpretation, insight, and belief. He goes on to say, however, that even when the content of our understanding is articulated explicitly, we understand it tacitly and, therefore, every statement of what we know is necessarily incomplete. "What the pupil must discover by an effort of his own," Polanyi says—and he could be talking as well of one learning to teach—"is something we could not tell him. And he knows it then in his turn but cannot tell it."

If we accept that conception of personal knowledge even provisionally, we can understand immediately why practicing teachers are so skeptical of the simple application of research or theory to practice. We can understand, too, why new teachers find it so difficult to take good advice. Any stipulation of effective practice is useless as a guide until it is informed by the knowing of the practitioner. I learned the same thing over and over again—without being able to explain it to myself—when I tried to apply my teachers' friendly advice in my own teaching.

One day at the University of Santa Clara, my Freshman English class was meeting in a room designed like a miniature amphitheater. A student stood up, gathered his things, walked down into the center of the well at the front of the room, and began going through the papers on my desk. I stopped talking to the whole class to ask him what he was doing. Class was almost over, he said accurately (it was five minutes before the hour), and he needed to pick up the handout I intended to distribute.

"Class is not over yet," I said deliberately. "I will hand out the assignment at the end."

The room was hushed. Nobody moved.

I now think I should have tried a different opening. I should have taken just a moment to find him the handout and let him go. It is difficult to unravel the motives that kept me from such conciliation. I had only five minutes of class left and did not want whatever we were doing interrupted. Then, too, I vaguely disliked him. His expression in class seemed regularly sullen to me. The way he slouched in his desk, one leg thrown over the chair in front of him, struck me as contemptuous. That *he* should have been the interruption, then, made me less flexible than I might otherwise have been. More intense still was my feeling of affront; those were *my* papers he was searching through; that was *my* desk; his rifling of my things felt rudely invasive. But the most important strand of my decision to resist him was my desire to maintain the control my unsmiling teachers had advised me to keep.

"It's time to go," he said, "and I need the assignment."

I was standing off to the side in the front of the room, very close to the first row of students. Because he was at my desk, he was standing behind me, his back to the class. When he spoke, he looked over his shoulder at me and then resumed his search through my papers.

I did not know what to do. Nothing in my training or experience had prepared me for this. We had both issued a challenge. I had no idea what to do next, but I made up one rule for myself on the spot: do not escalate.

Immediately I broke it.

"Class is not over," I said again. I kept my arms folded, hiding my hands.

"But *I* have to go," he said again, this time to my face.

We were unevenly matched in this skirmish. He was a freshman; I was "Dr. Murphy." I had the whole weight and authority of the university behind me. He stood alone. But he had plenty of grit, I could see that. Even as we were standing there, I envied him his recklessness. It was impossible for me. I had too much to lose. Every move I made was not simply a response to him; it was a performance. Without looking back, I knew that everyone in the room was watching me.

"That's fine. You may go," I imitated reasonableness, sureness.

"But I need the assignment."

I imitated authority and consistency: "You may get it next time."

Check. I gambled. I walked over to the door, held it open for him, and waited. I cannot say what I would have done if he had called my bluff, but he didn't. He left the papers at my desk, walked across the room, passed in front of me through the open door, and was gone.

Teaching is a live performance. Even with a script, it is mostly improvised. The simplest act is informed by a vast array of different, sometimes conflicting, concerns. My class plan notes might read merely "collect homework," "return papers," but as students begin to hand in their work, Angie asks, "What were we supposed to do?" Keith reminds me that he handed his in early. Chet and Vanessa exchange comments and giggle (I worry that they think the assignment was foolish busywork, what are they saying?). Gwyneth tries unsuccessfully to stifle a racking cough. I glance over, wave her toward the water fountain or the bathroom. How much class commotion is tolerable during this brief bureaucratic activity? (I am no longer anxious about that question, but I once worried a good deal that I might not be able to regain the students' attention.) Mike sits in the back corner, sullen. I told him yesterday that his work so far has been frivolous; today I try to resist the magnetic pull of his anger.

Those are just some of the strands of my experience related fairly directly to the business of the moment. They are braided with an infinite number of others more remote. Some are habits, assumptions, and memories I bring to teaching (a penchant for moving quickly in the room, for smiling; a hunch that small talk with students makes the classroom more hospitable for them; the image of Austin Fagothey's slender fingers straightening his history of philosophy lecture notes as he waited for us to settle into our desks). Some strands are outside teaching as such but color the moment vividly: listening to Brahms this morning instead of getting up at the first click of the alarm, the gutters cracking and rusting on the garage roof, the cardinal in the pear tree by the back porch, a migraine. "What were we supposed to do?" Angie asks. Her question annoys, amuses, wearies, us, perplexes us, knocks us off balance, seems perfectly easy to answer.

Polanyi is right. What we know even about the simplest acts we perform as teachers is largely inexpressible. That is one of the reasons why, once we seem to have learned how to teach, we find it difficult to say what we have learned. It is why many of us never feel we have learned enough. It is why we are reticent about sadness and joy.

Standing at the board, chalk in hand, ready to write the name "Polonius" up next to "Ophelia" and "Laertes," a teacher suddenly sees herself from the outside. She notices her wool skirt, remembers the feel of the green plaid uniform against her legs when she first studied *Hamlet* in the eleventh grade, how the pleats fell open across her lap, wonders how long it will take her student Scott to come up with the character's name that she is ready to write, waits for him to think, watches herself waiting, is amazed to see herself there in front of a college classroom, can't imagine how it happened that she is there, can't remember ever thinking that teaching in college would require waiting for a student who hadn't read the assignment to guess about the name of a major character, regrets asking, feels foolish with the chalk poised there, feels also sluggish, numb, as if she were no longer in control of the class, as if she were no longer involved but merely looking on, a disinterested spectator.

At 1:45 on a gray November afternoon, the fourth-grade children are rambunctious. Their substitute teacher (we all feel like substitute teachers some days) tries to calculate what remains of the promise of the day. An art lesson in which the class has just made turkey collages produced stuff for the bulletin board, a floor covered with scraps of colored construction paper, and glue on both faucets of the sink. The plans the regular teacher left on her desk say it is time for reading and writing, though how anyone could imagine doing reading or writing now is difficult to say. The room is sweltering. The custodian has been in and out of the classroom since 11:00 trying to adjust the radiator. If the high wooden windows were not sealed shut, the substitute teacher would throw them all open and stand with the children gratefully in their fresh draft. For a moment he considers telling everyone to bundle up and taking them all outside to the playground for an unorthodox recess, but then he remembers the difficulty he had getting them back to the room after lunch and loses heart. These are not his children, after all. This is not his classroom. He does not know what to do. He cannot say what will work. But even before the children are finished putting away scissors and paper and glue, he reaches into his utility bag and takes out a rosewood flute.

None of my teachers or colleagues told me this when I began to teach, or if they told me I did not understand, but such moments are at the center of every teacher's life. Learning to teach is something more than acquiring prescriptions of good practice. Even if we have a binder full of fail-safe ("research-based," "field-tested") teaching ideas, we will not be able to use it without feeling fake. And there are no guarantees. Teaching is full of doubt, helplessness, and ignorance. There is no learning it by heart. It is a personal act, new every time, essentially uncertain and thus every time creative.

When I finally figured out that John Wilson was calling out "Here" for everyone in my class at Moreau High School, I did not know what to do. I decided to walk down along his row and call the names from his desk. That worked, but it did not keep him from other diversions—answering all my questions before anyone else could speak; raising his hand (when I asked him to do that in the hope that it would control his talking out) and keeping it raised for the entire class period; gasping or sighing at other students' halting answers; putting his head down on the desk (when I asked him not to criticize his classmates) and imitating loud snores. If the class did not appreciate his arrogance, they loved his endless inventiveness.

I loved his directness. When he was not trying to distract me or the other students with some entertainment, he looked straight at me. He watched my thoughts forming. "How does Steinbeck make the pearl destructive?" I would ask, and then clarify it by rephrasing: "What parts of the story seem to be included for the purpose of showing the danger of the pearl for Kino?" Before I had finished, John would not only have some answer; he would have jumped ahead to the implication: that the dangers shown in the novel are all external, but they imply an internal threat as well. I would speak and see John looking at me, looking into me.

He was smart and quick. In midyear, he fought with his parents—I can imagine now the difficulty of being his father—left home, found a place to stay. One weekend he helped Susie and me move into our first house. That evening we ate fried chicken on top of the cardboard moving boxes. He said, "Have you ever made love on the kitchen floor?" Precocious, irrepressible, he continued to disrupt the class, in spite of my trying to control him with after-school penalty hall. As sure as his understanding was of the work I was assigning, he did very little of it and that little was poor. His grades in my class were uniformly lousy.

"Why, John?" I finally asked. "I don't understand this."

"I don't know," he said.

"You have at least as good a grasp of this stuff as anyone else in the class . . ." (I meant *better*, but I did not want to denigrate anyone else's ability or effort in trying to help him.) " . . . Why are your grades so poor? You must just not be studying at all."

"I'm not." The usual directness. "What we're doing is so easy, I can't stand it. It's ridiculous. That's why I keep farting around in class."

His explanation immediately seemed true. And refreshing. "Then let's do something different."

We struck a deal on the spot: John would come to class every day and not goof around; if he wanted to make a contribution, he could do so, but he could not hog the floor; the rest of his regular work for the semester would be canceled. In place of the ordinary tenth-grade curriculum, he would read Plato's *Republic*; we would talk about it in occasional tutorials outside of class; when he was ready, he would take an essay examination on the whole book.

A hare-brained scheme. I do not know what inspired it. Boredom and frustration, certainly, and at least some intellectual pretense on my part. Whatever its source, John said, "OK, deal."

And it was. He read, *I* read (I had not stopped to think that I was signing myself up, too). We talked. I made up the exam for him, and he wrote wonderfully clear essay answers. I wish I had kept his essays, but all I have are some of the questions from which he could choose, scribbled on a small piece of notepaper, preserved in my copy of Plato.

It was the only essay exam I think I gave during my first year of teaching. I did not know how to construct an essay exam. My other tests that year were objective, made up of multiple-choice, matching, true-and-false, and fill-in-the-blank questions, a format I borrowed from my new colleagues and that I thought fitting for the grade and the material. In the Plato exam, however, I was imitating my college teachers. I wrote it under the mixed influence of Austin Fagothey, my history of philosophy professor, and all the instructors of my college literature courses. That was what I thought they had expected of me, and that was what I thought I should expect of John.

It was an impersonation. But it was something more, too: an act of radical improvisation.

"Have you ever made love on the kitchen floor?" he asked.

"Have you ever read Plato?" I asked.

Then for weeks in the evening, after I had done my other homework—prepared lesson plans for the next day, written out Ditto masters, corrected student papers, tended our infant son, Kevin—I sat in the green, flea-market chair by the front window of our new house and read. Socrates: "I must have recourse to fiction, and put together a figure made up of many things." And every day, from the back of the classroom, John would look at me and listen and finish my sentences with his eyes.

5

Syllabus

ENGLISH 101—Introduction to Expository Writing
Three hours lecture
Prerequisite: None

This course will provide students with an introduction to
the basic principles of the composing process, rhetoric,
and standard usage. Through a number of expository
writing assignments, students will be taught to write to
specific audiences to accomplish particular rhetorical purposes, e.g., to inform, to offer an opinion, to present an
analysis.

THIS IS THE current catalogue description for the first semester of Freshman English at Radford University. Sixty-plus
people are assigned to teach almost a hundred sections of English 101 every fall semester. Recently the department has developed some guidelines for the course that are more specific than
the catalogue description, but even they give individual teachers
great latitude in determining the shape, activity, and focus of
their particular sections. The syllabi we hand out the first day of
class say different things. The courses we teach do different
things. Prospective students imagine that Freshman English is
something clearly defined. It isn't.

My own course description contains no provision for lecture. Nor does it promise to provide students with "the" basic
principles of anything. One recent semester, for example, it detailed the textbooks (the *Harbrace College Handbook* and
Donald Hall's *Writer's Reader*), requirements (among others:

ten two- to three-page essays, an idea journal, freewriting), and stipulations (for instance, regular attendance in class and careful participation in writing groups). On subsequent pages, it expanded on essay topics, the assigned journal, individual conferences with me, and grades, and concluded with what I hoped would be an inspirational "Note on the Course."

What my syllabus or course description doesn't say is what often actually happens—how the stipulations turn the requirements into a penal code, how the grading procedures make my exhortations about personal value seem bogus, how the entire course may come down to moments, perhaps a single lucky moment, of illumination.

Not only do my course descriptions differ from the catalogue's and from my colleagues'; they differ from other syllabi I have written for the same course at different times. Every time I teach 101, I do it differently. Every time, I reconsider and reconstruct the course. I reinterpret the general catalogue designation in a concretely new way. Each time I embark on the course—having prepared for it by charting its progress and laying in detailed provisions—the actual passage requires so many adjustments that I have come to wonder why I insist on making plans in the first place.

I have not yet been able to persuade myself to settle for a syllabus as brief as the catalogue description, but I am trying to make do these days with one page: here are the books, the due dates, the number of essays, and the grading procedures; I will explain the rest as the semester proceeds. Such a summary is at least compact and no more ambiguous than my past attempts at comprehensiveness, which ended up loose and misleading.

The disadvantage is that I am afraid students will think I don't know what I'm doing. I want my course to sound serious and thoughtful; I want to seem so myself. I do not want to appear to be throwing the thing together at the last minute, hoping to figure it out as we go along. But, of course, the truth is that in a sense that is exactly what I do. For all my planning, I always watch the actual development of a course in progress to gauge whether what the students and I are doing is working and whether what comes next really fits with what has been happening. In practice, my plans are simply provisional. What happens is always different either from what I expected or from what, in my syllabus, I seemed to describe.

For example, I usually ask students in 101 to choose their own topics for essays. Persuasive arguments can be made for and against such a policy, just as a strong case could be made for assigning some topics and leaving students some choice of others. At different times, I have tried almost all variations on the theme. But when I ask students to determine the topics for their essays themselves, I urge them to choose topics they care about. I tell them that I think they will write best—with the most clarity, force, and conviction—if they write to communicate something they really want and mean to say.

I believe that advice. But one semester, when the first essays came in, I realized (again) that it was not enough. The thing many freshmen care most about at the beginning of their first semester in college is the absolutely disruptive experience of *being* there. Many cannot make immediate sense of it. My suggestion that they choose topics they care about, then, can inadvertently mislead.

Here is how two of their essays began:

Adjusting to College Life

The point of this paper was partly for my own benefit, it was also out of believing, hey, maybe there are other people who feel this way, and are fearful of college, overwhelmed with all the work.

College can be overwhelming, and it was to me. With all the new situations, and responsibilities there are. With papers to write, and so many books to read. Getting to know new people, and letting them know who you are, it can be really scarey!

Radford a Major Change in My Life
That Will Prepare Me For the Future

Everyone has to go through transformations throughout their life. My coming to Radford was a major change in my life. In my opinion Radford is a change in my life that will prepare me for the future. It will prepare me to be on my own and it will also prepare me for a job. When I first arrived here I was totally bewildered, until now I had never been away from home for a long period of time. At first this was hard to get use to. Leaving home is just a part of growing up. Everyone has to leave home sooner or later. My advice to an individual who is thinking of college is to go. College will prepare you to be on your own and for an occupation.

I do not remember the writer of this second paragraph, but every time I reread his essay I am struck by its hollowness. General lead: "Everyone has to go through transformations in their life." Personal perspective: "My coming to Radford was a major change in my life." Audience: "an individual who is thinking of college." Main idea: "My advice is to go. College will prepare you to be on your own and for an occupation." The student's "transformation" is still going on. It is "a major change" he hopes will be worth it, but the accounts are not even close to being settled yet, so his advice is wooden and his language pathetically unconvincing. When I read the paragraph, it seems to me the writer would have been better served if I had given him a specific assignment, a personal response, say, to Doris Lessing's short story "Through the Tunnel." As it is, I asked him to find and develop a topic he cared about, and his doing so disabled him.

In "Adjusting to College Life," the trauma of the subject is up on the surface of the language, explicit even in the first word of the title. This is experience under way; the writer is adjusting even as she writes. Which words will do? "Hey." "Overwhelming." "Scarey." She slips once into the past tense, saying that college "was" overwhelming for her, but everywhere else her fragility is present and palpable. So much so that it astonishes, unsettles me even now. She writes without protection, flays her feeling and holds it up for us to see. I ask students to write honestly, but I don't mean *this*. "I'm an English teacher," I want to say. "This is school. Don't trust us this much."

I remember her. When I tried to tell her that her words were misspelled and her sentences fragmented, she smiled shyly and nodded.

"And your paragraphs," I forced myself to go on and say, "they're somewhat random. The parts of your story are jumbled."

61

"Yes," she said, as if she knew.

There was no explaining the failures of her paper. She was encouraged to come to college by people who loved her. The last Friday at work, her fellow workers gave her a surprise party and eighty dollars for books. She rode the Trailways bus alone up from North Carolina to Radford. Then she wrote an essay for Freshman English full of sentences like this: "All these things I have written, I did so to let you know who I am, and to say, 'Hey!, It's okay to be afraid, you're sure not alone, I guess I found that out just today!'" I told her I couldn't grade her essay. She said she understood.

The catalogue description for English 101 is so reticent that it not only makes no mention of either of those two writers; it denies them. My syllabus complies. It pretends that the course hums along, well tooled, right into Christmas. Fifteen weeks, three days a week.

When I construct the syllabus, I put the calendar of the semester on a sheet of legal-sized scratch paper, then block in those days when student essays will be due. One recent semester, papers were to be submitted every Monday for ten weeks, Labor Day to Thanksgiving, then one revision every Monday for three weeks between Thanksgiving and Christmas. Having marked the due dates on my scratch sheet, I worked backwards. Mondays were for submitting finished papers and beginning to work up subjects for the next week. Wednesdays I devoted to a variety of activities—perhaps in-class writing, during which I walked around the room and individually conferred with students who wanted to talk with me about their writing; short exercises to help students analyze and write introductions or conclusions or to compose sentences with greater density, vividness, and precision; sometimes reading publicly and appreciating selected passages of their classmates' writing. Fridays were always scheduled for small-group discussions of drafts of the students' essays in progress. Every week.

When I require students to discuss drafts of their papers in groups, I ask explicitly for a "complete and substantial" draft so they don't write simply a handful of possible ideas. I sometimes ask them to bring a photocopy for me, assuming that my seeing it will make their doing a thorough draft more likely. The photocopies for fellow group members are to permit them to read along while the writer is reading aloud. But none of those prescriptions guarantees that groups will work as described, and I am always surprised at how differently the students are prepared.

One has a draft but no copies ("The copier in the library was broken"). One has a six-page manuscript in tiny print that will take probably twenty minutes to read aloud, maybe more, enough to swamp a good half of the class time the group has available to apportion to four papers. One student says she brought some notes ("I was thinking of writing about my grandmother. She died when I was seven. She collected a lot of different kinds of things. We used to visit her every year, but then she went into the hospital. What do you think about that? Do you think I could write a paper about her?"). One has nothing ("I still have a lot of work to do, but I was thinking about writing about my experience as an Army brat, about the embassy parties, about all the different countries, about always being chaperoned by Marines and everything").

The group discussions surprise as well. I came to a group in the center of the room one day, asked as usual if I could join them, and when they said yes, pulled up an empty desk and sat down. Silence. No one seemed to want to volunteer any comment. So I asked around the group, one at a time, if they had read and discussed their drafts. Yes. I asked if they had any questions still unanswered that they would like me to talk with them about. No. I asked what their drafts were about, and one by one they told me, briefly.

Somewhere during this forced exchange, I noticed that Mary's draft of her paper about her roommate was resting on top of a large open textbook, so large that its printed pages stuck out beyond the pages of the draft. Under Angela's papers was an open notebook. By the time I had climbed over the intervening rows of desks to join a different group by the windows, the two of them were already talking animatedly again about biology, their two partners waiting in silence for the class period to end. I felt partly responsible for the charade. I had invited myself into their group and forced them to pretend that they wanted to be discussing drafts of their papers. The talk I compelled from them was insincere, and before I was done with it (my eye on those biology notes) my talk was insincere as well. Writing groups in English 101 do not always work that way. After studying their operation in practice, one researcher, Sarah Freedman, suggests that they promote a wide range of different experiences. But her findings correspond to my own observations: writing groups often do not work as neatly as the syllabus implies. I may devote a third of the semester to student talk in class about their writing and still have to admit that it is sometimes a dismal waste. Sometimes, however, such talk occasions striking, poignant moments—surprises of a different order.

A group of students asked once if they could move their meeting somewhere else. The classroom was too noisy, they said. Could they meet in the lounge of their dorm? I said sure. I would join them there. The class met at five o'clock in the evening. By the time I got to Stuart lounge, it was already dark outside and many dorm residents were at dinner across campus in one of the dining halls. The group had the room to itself, spread out in a wide circle on couches and easy chairs. They had become comfortable with one another and decided easily who would read. The first paper I heard recounted the story of the writer's high school graduation trip to the beach (*every* semester at Radford, given a choice of topics, some freshman students will write about their graduation trips to the beach). Her essay was about a guy she had met there and had been thinking about since, about how they swam together and went out to dinner and walked in the evening barefoot on the sand. The story was genial, thoughtless.

I said, "May I ask you a question?"

"Sure."

I: "Is your paper about a guy you really met or is it about someone you wish you had?"

She: "Well, I did meet him . . ."

"I'm sorry," I said. "I didn't mean that. I mean are you describing who he actually was or what you'd like him to have been?"

Pause. She pulled her legs up under herself on the couch, looked down at her paper. "We really went out . . . but it didn't happen exactly like this."

I: "I know it's none of my business, but was it good? The date?"

She: "It was OK."

I: "And so you're writing here about how you wish it had been . . . ?"

She: "Yes."

The room shrank; our circle contracted. "Then why do you write about him like this? You're talking about something very important here—the kind of person you want to become friends with. But you hardly talk about him at all. You've got prawns at the Happy Anchor here. And lights on the boardwalk. People night fishing for shark on the pier. Moonlight. Bare toes in the sand. But there's no person here. It seems to me that what you've got here is the surface of a sort of TV romance. Why not be more daring? Why not talk about love?"

I might have been speaking only for myself, but as it turned out I wasn't. In the hush of that large, deserted dormitory lounge, it was as if the word "love" spoke for us all. Everyone in the group began to move, to talk at once, to agree, to share their own stories of "OK" dates at the beach, to say how the clichés of romance can thin the feelings we most value. If the paper were going to admit its purpose, to try to draw the person she *wanted* him to be, what would it say? What might this girl and boy have talked about as they walked? What words might have silenced them? Not, what was the light like in the surf, but what was the light like in them? Some extraordinary change had come over the group. We were all convinced there for the moment that it was literally *possible*—however unexpected—to write a paper in school about love.

It is just as unlikely, and just as possible, to write about love's cruelty.

I joined another group another semester just after Thanksgiving, this time in a classroom crowded with noisy groups. A young woman was reading the revised draft of an essay about Christmas morning at her family's home. When she finished reading, she opened her notebook, slipped her essay in, sat back with folded arms, and then, not before, looked up at us. Daring us to say anything. No one but me seemed willing to take up the challenge.

"That's wonderful, Stacey," I said. "What a powerful point you make." I think I was smiling as I spoke. I certainly felt the truth of my reaction. But I also felt its strangeness in the face of her fierce stare. I went on.

"*Everyone* is going to be mouthing the clichéd criticism of Christmas spirit—materialism, loss of spiritual values, etc., etc. —but your approach is fresh and frank. And, because your testimony is so personal, it's irresistible."

Stacey sat silent, motionless. I looked around the group. They were waiting.

"I think you could strengthen your essay even more, though . . ." I said, "if you gave us more details of your family's Christmas morning, if you showed us how different it is from the stereotyped picture we get from Hallmark and Macy's. The draft you read to us is already very suggestive, but if you want to make the case for all of us that Christmas isn't what we pretend it is, some more description might reinforce the effect of your point."

I suppose that the other students in Stacey's group had no more inkling of what was coming than I, but they had more tact.

"What do you mean when you say that you and your sister always fight?" I asked.

Her answer was immediate, clipped.

"She wants to go down early and I want to sleep in."

"How does that turn into a fight?"

"Our mom gets into it."

I wanted her to say more.

"What do you mean? What do you do? What does your sister do? And your mom?"

Stacey looked down at her desk: "When I don't get up, my sister yells at me. Then she goes downstairs to the kitchen and complains to my parents. I don't know. She comes upstairs, comes in my room. I tell her to get out. She slams the door and shouts downstairs that I still won't get up. My mom calls to me."

None of that was in the paper. I was no longer prompting her. Stacey was talking to herself.

"My sister yells, 'The slut *won't* get up . . .' 'Slut?' my father says from the kitchen. 'SLUT?' My mother hollers up to me, 'Stacey, get *up*. It's Christmas *morning*.' 'I told you, the girl's a slut,' my sister shouts down at them. Then my father starts in on her and on my mother both: 'Will you two stop screaming, for Christsake!' I wrap myself in the bedspread and walk out on the landing and all three of them turn on me."

Pause.

"What do you say to each other?" I asked.

"I don't know . . . Everything."

Not knowing what more to say, I went on anyway.

"And then you open Christmas presents together?"

"No. We each get our own from under the tree and take them to our bedrooms and open them there."

"And that's Christmas Day—alone in your rooms?"

"Yes," she said. She was crying now. "Until the company comes for Christmas dinner."

We sat in silence for a while together. Stacey kept looking down, her arms still folded, locked against her chest, ignoring the tears. I could not assess the damage I had done. I did not try to comfort her. I went on as if this were an ordinary event in a writing class.

"That's a powerful story, Stacey. It may be so painful you'll decide not to write it, but if you want to, and if you can, you will say something deeply true about Christmas for all of us."

I did not know how to end, how to free her, how to give them permission to go on to someone else's paper.

"Thank you," was all I could think to say. If she had looked at me, I would have tried to reach out to her somehow with my eyes.

Sometimes in English 101, my meetings with students are in private, in individual conferences I arrange to hold with them in my office. Usually I require a minimum number of such conferences, say two for each student during the semester. But I also encourage students to schedule as many additional appointments as we both have time for. What my syllabus doesn't say—and no one will automatically infer—is that some afternoons there are students coming to my office until past dark. I try not to run late, but the conversation with one student can snarl up and stretch five, eight minutes over the allotted time, and I will never catch up. It is not obvious in the syllabus that when I pack the conference times together, twenty or thirty minutes each for four or five hours on five consecutive days, I have to disconnect my office phone and no one who has not signed up will be able to get in to see me.

One day a young man came to my office door, saw that I was busy with another student, and sat down on the floor in the hall to wait. After some time, a second student came along and sat down with him. The first had no appointment. He was enrolled in one of my two literature classes. He knew nothing about my scheduled conferences for Freshman English. The second student was early for his conference. When I was finished talking with the woman in my office, both people waiting had a claim to be next, and in fact the second courteously offered to defer to the first. As much as I appreciated the impulse of his offer, it couldn't solve the problem. By arranging my time so closely I had made it impossible to meet with this other student until the next week.

He couldn't understand it or, if he understood it, couldn't believe it.

"You're my *teacher*," he said. "I'm enrolled in your course. What do you *mean* you can't see me until next Tuesday? I've been waiting here *already* for going on a half hour." I apologized, tried to explain, said I'd be glad to meet with him the first day I had any open time. This didn't satisfy him. I felt the clock ticking on the waiting student's conference. With one last apology, I cut off our futile talk and invited the other young man in.

When I schedule marathon conferences like this, the dimensions of normal time distort. The coffee cooks thick in the pot. My nerves grow more alert. The air in the room becomes electric. Days full of conferences exhaust me, but that is because they concentrate my attention so. My office mate comes and goes; his students come and go; I do not notice. The words on the page at the corner of my desk, the look on the writer's face, the pauses in his talk about what he was trying to do in the writing—these are everything.

So I don't really know how long it was before I found that student at my door again, and it took me some moments to understand what the piece of paper he thrust at me was for. "Sign," he said, peremptorily.

We were standing in the doorway of my office. He was holding out his blue Bic ballpoint pen for me to use.

"I'm dropping your class," he said. "The dean gave me permission. He told me to get your signature there."

Dropping? The dean? I must have just been blinking stupidly at him.

"I'm paying for these courses I'm taking. I expect to be able to get in to see my teachers in their offices."

I held the drop slip in the palm of my hand and initialed the "Instructor" line. When I gave back the pen and the signed form, he walked away without saying anything more. I shook my head a little, to clear it, and welcomed the next student on my list with the warmest greeting I could manage.

There is no trace of that day in my syllabus, nor of the day Sandra Miyoshi was last on the list of appointments. While we were talking about the draft of her story, a campus police officer had come by, checked all the office doors, poked his head around the jamb to smile and say good night, and switched off the corridor light at the end of the hall. Sandra and I went on talking about her paper.

It was about her grandmother in Hawaii. The old woman's parents had emigrated from Japan with her when she was still just a child. From her grandmother's allusions to it, Sandra guessed that the move had been unhappy for her, but she was not sure why. So she was writing about it, trying to imagine a possible story. There was a young boy in her village. Sandra made him her grandmother's cousin (this was no story of infatuation). In the evenings, the two children worked on their knees, weeding the family garden.

On the night before she left, the boy slipped a small package into Sandra's grandmother's young hand. It was wrapped in newsprint and tied with string. She put it in her pocket. Neither of them spoke. Only when she was already on the train to Kyoto did she allow herself to tear the corner off the wrapping to look. Silk. Violet. She touched it with her fingertips.

Sandra's paper lay between us on the corner of the wooden desk. As she read to me from it, bowed over its pages, long lines of her blue-black hair rested on its white surface. Our talk ranged over many different things—the structure of her sentences, questions of detail (Was the family's leaving a secret? Were they *fleeing?*), how much to tell of the earlier relationship between the young cousins. At one pause, Sandra looked at me, channeled her hair back behind one ear. "You're the first teacher I've ever had who listened to me," she said.

I did not quarrel with her exaggeration. The happiness I felt at her thanking me so is indistinguishable from the awe I still feel watching her silk scarf ripple in my memory.

Violet, lavender, lime, orange, its fictional colors wild against the pale blue Pacific sky. The girl in Sandra's story ran along the beach trailing the scarf behind her, looking over her shoulder at its exquisite plumage, making great arcs of color in the sun. She held it to her cheek. She knotted it around her wrists. She stood in the surf, her sandals in one hand, the scarf in the other, alternately looking down to where its tip floated in the foam at her ankles and up over the red volcano rim behind Honolulu toward the east.

The syllabus for English 101 is as much a fiction as Sandra's story. It contains nothing about wasted time or suffering, about plans unrealized, surprises, missed connections, unexpected disappointment and success. In one sense, then, the syllabus is a performance—a masque. I appear to be articulating the format, rules, and content of the course. But what I am doing in fact is expressing my hope.

6

Personal Essays

PHILIP ARCA'S FATHER was a cop. He drove around town alone in a squad car. His leather gun holster squeaked. Philip began an essay called "Sharing the Night Together" like this:

> My mom is nearing the end of her nightly vigil. He should be home any minute now. It's 12:45. If he got off work at midnight and finished up his paperwork and drove home right away he would be home in about ten minutes. She can never sleep when he works these hours. It's worse when he has dogwatch, even for me. The house is off limits during the day because Dad is catching up on his sleep. My friends and I have to play down the street.
>
> I hear the opening of a cupboard and the clank of a peanut butter jar top. Mom eats anything that'll coat her worried, acid-ridden stomach. I've seen her gulp down Maalox like fraternity boys chug beer. A car rumbles down the street. My mom scurries to the kitchen window and lifts up the shade. False alarm. She sits down and finishes her inch-thick peanut butter sandwich and creamy glass of buttermilk. Tomorrow morning I'll find a knife gooey with peanut butter and a glass coated with curdled buttermilk in the sink; remnants of her nightwatch.

Imagine all the facts Philip knew about his parents, all the details of gesture and voice with which he became familiar as he was growing up. Consider the millions of bits of information, all the incidents in this boy's life that might serve as the subject of an autobiographical essay. Including all the moments as innocuous as this one (nothing special happened; his father came home and went to bed), how many will there be? If nothing else, then, "Sharing the Night Together" is an awesome act of selection.

But more than selection. Compression, too. Every detail counts: the imaginative rehearsal of the father's routine—clocking off, paperwork, drive home; "dogwatch"; kids at play while the man with the deadly profession sleeps; peanut butter and Maalox; his mom's scurrying; the window shade; the sounds of waiting—clank, rumble. Nothing is irrelevant, nothing labored. The ironies seem natural. Ulcerous worry set against innocent play. The remnants of a mother's night watch in the sink, her son's on the page. Even the title comes to be charged with secret meaning: since the boy lay awake in the dark, he too shared.

When people ask what I do, I say I teach writing and then can hardly resist qualifying. "I teach academic writing," I say, "essay writing, exposition." I teach the general introductory college course in composition, the course required of almost all students entering American colleges. But most questioners want to know whether I teach creative writing, short stories, poetry, journalism, or what is being called these days literary nonfiction. As soon as I say no—and I almost always do; I have no good term for the writing I teach—I deny one of the things I most deeply believe about my work.

To distinguish exposition from short stories and poetry and nonfiction journalism on the ground that it is not creative writing is to misdescribe it. Essentially. All writing—whether lyric or lab report—is creative to the extent that it shapes words, data, arguments into meaning. I learned that from poet Josephine Miles, who reminds us that "com-position" is the act of putting things together. To draw a sharp line between fiction and nonfiction, therefore, is to misrepresent both. Essays are not about a real world, stories about an imagined. Both are imagined worlds composed from the materials of the real.

I ask students in my Freshman English course to do many different kinds of writing. Freewriting—a fast, uncritical record of the student's stream of thought, often written in class and which I first learned about from reading Ken Macrorie and Peter Elbow. Journal writing—not a personal diary but a series of informal reflections on the student's writing or reading in this class or some other, writing used pragmatically to help the student learn. An essay developing a thesis statement (which I first learned to understand and present to students from Brother John Perron at Moreau High School). A book review, an in-class essay exam, an essay based on research, a short story—sometimes all of them, sometimes a selection, sometimes still others.

But the staple assignment of my Freshman English course is the essay of personal experience. I ask students to choose a moment of memory that they regard as significant and to recount it in its most vivid and essential details. I ask them to address their essay to an audience, some person they know or can imagine, some group of readers they want their experience to move or instruct. Though it has some parameters, this is an open assignment. It may include narrative, character description, dialogue, commentary. It may focus on a person or place, an object or an incident. It may frame its account of experience with an idea or leave the idea largely implicit, embedded in the representation of the experience. It may strike different kinds of personal notes: confessional, meditative, reasoned, polemical.

It is a very difficult assignment. Difficult to explain, for one thing. The words I use need definition—what is an essay? which are the essential details? how long is a moment and what makes it significant?—and my definitions tend to be circular. I point to examples: Philip Arca's essay, pieces of my own writing, bits of freewriting from the students in the class, Beth Gutshall's account of the sound of her father's slippers in the hospital corridors when he was recovering from a kidney transplant. The more examples I can give the better because then students are less likely to think the assignment has only one proper form. Still, they find it extremely difficult to write, and no wonder. The difficulty derives not merely from the assignment or from my inadequate explanation of it, but from the mysteriously creative act of writing itself.

One of the examples I give students to read is E. B. White's frequently anthologized essay "Once More to the Lake," the story of a fishing trip White took with his young son. Together they return to the Maine lake where White spent his childhood summers. Now middle-aged, he finds that everything is the same as he remembered, and different. The man and the boy sleep in the same cabin among the same pine trees. They walk along the same track up to the camp house for meals. In the store they find the same candies and pop. The fishing, the boats, the sounds of the woods, the afternoon thunderstorms—all become a montage of memory superimposed on the present, so that White cannot tell sometimes whether he is the father or the son.

In thirteen paragraphs, his essay evokes summer's timeless pleasures: still mornings, sunshine, sugar doughnuts, sarsaparilla. Even as those pleasures are itemized, however, and savored again, it is in the mind of a man looking back. Even as they are made vivid in his memory, they are understood to be past, lost. The chill one feels in the groin when pulling on a wet bathing suit is simply cold for the boy. For his father, it is the chill of death. Alternating between past and present, White manages to make them merge for us as they did for him. Because he is able to hold both simultaneously—the sweetness and the chill—he is able to imbue each with the feeling of the other. Every single thing he rediscovers at the lake—moss and watermelon and the moonlit thoughts of girls—is shadowed by his growing old. Yet even the shock of death itself is lightened by the happiness of his summertime youth.

"Do *that*," I say, meaning "or your version of it."

"But we don't have children," I hear someone say.

"No, but you have parents."

I feel the frail hand of my father in mine as we stumble down a forgotten hill in distant woods.

"But my father's an accountant," a student says, still perplexed by my explanation, "not a policeman. Nobody worries about him."

"OK," I say, and there in the lurid blue lines of my father's face I see again the tiring of his heart.

"I don't mean do that *exactly*. I don't mean write an essay about waiting for your father to come home from work or about getting drenched in a summer rainstorm. I mean pick a moment of experience that was important to you and write about why. Let the writing help you understand its meaning."

"But I don't *know* what it means."

I want to tell them to be patient, that its meaning will unfold. I am tempted to say that if they enter deeply enough into the moment they will discover everything they know and care about concentrated there. But I say neither. I know that the secret of the meaning is not in the moment, but in them, in their mind's construing past and present. I do not know how to say that. No one knows how we compose meanings with such force that they seem, even to us who make them, found.

The real subject of Freshman English is the act of writing. The imaginative and rational act of composing. The practical act of using equipment, gathering material, and constructing ideas in a purposeful written text. The essay of personal experience can serve as the focal assignment in such a course because in it the writer creates the meaning of his or her experience. Whatever its subject or form, all written composition shares this central creativity. When a geology teacher asks for an essay about magma on a final exam, she is making a creative assignment. Whatever the specific focus of her question, the students' principal task is to select relevant facts from what they know and relate them to each other in a significant whole. The answer to the question lies not in the facts (which are a memorized given) but in the whole (which the students themselves must create). When an engineer writes a letter on behalf of his clients petitioning the county for a regulation waiver, he must decide not only what information to include and how much, but in what order and with what degree of servility.

Academic writing, business writing, science or technical writing—all are as composed as poems or stories. Data are chosen, not simply reported. Jargon itself is elective. Writing—even about facts—breaks what philosopher Paul Ricoeur calls the "prestige of fact." That is one of the fundamental themes of Freshman English as I understand it.

Even professional writers, however, sometimes misdescribe their art. In *The Journalist and the Murderer*, for example, essayist Janet Malcolm suggests that the writer's critical act is in *finding* a compelling subject. The crucial requirement of powerful nonfiction portraiture, she claims, lies in seizing on subjects who have already made themselves interesting, who have already "auto-fictionalized" themselves—people like Perry Smith, the murderer of Truman Capote's *In Cold Blood*. According to Malcolm, Capote simply reported the "ready-made literary figure" he had had the luck to turn up. But in her explanation, Malcolm confuses the process with the product. The Perry Smith of *In Cold Blood* is so finely realized that he feels more like a person than a character. But in fact he is the product of Capote's wonderful imaginative selection and compression. The elements of Perry's portrait—his breakfasts of Pall Mall cigarettes and root beer; the striking pain in his crippled and deformed legs; a grueling fight with his down-and-out father over a crust of bread; being beaten as a child in an orphanage by a flashlight-wielding nun; the twisted sympathy of his attempt to protect one of his teenage victims from his braggart partner; these and many others—are combined to create a protagonist of extraordinary pathos. That is, Capote *created* Perry Smith; he didn't simply find him.

Malcolm herself seems finally to agree. After they have invented themselves, she says, the fabulous characters of nonfiction must get under the skin of the writer. Only then is their literary transformation possible. But in conceding that they are transformed, Malcolm acknowledges that even ready-made subjects are remade in the process of writing. This is always the way, in stories or essays, about murder or philosophy: exposition is creative. Because it is composed, even nonfiction is fiction.

Among some rhetoricians and composition theorists these days the personal essay assignment is in disfavor. One of its most appealing virtues, that it allows students to write about what they know best, is being turned against it. The personal essay, some critics say, fosters narcissism by permitting students to focus narrowly on themselves rather than expanding their understanding of the world. Another virtue is its democratic impulse. Everyone has personal experience to render and interpret; there are no privileged experiences. But that too is being challenged. The personal essay, some critics say, is just one more institutional assignment; its alleged valuing of student experience, therefore, is either naive or duplicitous. For critics who emphasize the importance of what are being called "discourse communities" and the special rhetorical demands of different social contexts, the personal essay assignment has yet other weaknesses. It seems to give students an artificial and misleading autonomy, permitting them to write free of the constraints that other teachers, disciplines, or audiences will impose. In the view of some critics, the personal essay also gives writers too much authority. It implies that the meaning of their rendered experience is their own to compose, that it can be fixed by them, that it is not subject as well to the audience's construction in reading.

Though the formulation of some of those objections is new, the personal writing assignment has been subject to criticism since it was introduced into American composition classrooms more than a hundred years ago. According to historian Robert Connors, both the criticism and the assignment are likely to continue. Teachers have always been uncomfortable, Connors says, with the prospect of an educational system "producing students whose only coherent subject matter [is] themselves and their experiences." At the same time, personal experience writing has "remained the central core of many of the essays students are asked to do, and the original impulse—to make writing meaningful to student writers—has never disappeared."

I share the impulse. I want writing to be meaningful for students in English 101. I also feel the discomfort. I think that is why I assign other kinds of writing besides the essay of personal experience. But I am not persuaded by the objections. I know that personal essays can be foolish, arid stuff. Every semester someone writes a paper about what she and her friends did first, then next, on their graduation trip to Myrtle Beach. Two or three pages on the time of their lives. The car broke down. There were cockroaches in the motel. They got gorgeous tans, met some great people. The subject is not the problem here; neither is the information. What such writing lacks is a meaning that makes the subject significant, a meaning that the information is shaped to compose. Just one of the paradoxical features of the Myrtle Beach story is that students themselves admit that it is dull. They don't want to write it (even though the trip was great and they chose the subject themselves); they don't want to read it. But their admission does not help them. The assignment is to render the moment meaningfully, and everyone who reads the essay knows they have not done so yet.

Writing about a family nightwatch as Philip Arca did, however, is a manifest achievement. In remembering and then rendering those details of his childhood, Philip had to recreate his mother and father, even himself. Choosing what to include was an act of creative imagination. Describing his father walking down the hall and into his son's dark room, the leather belt squeaking as he leaned over the bed—Philip caught the curve not only of habit but of understanding and love. "Good night, buddy," his father would say, and Philip knew that his father knew that now finally he could sleep.

Writing an essay of personal experience is like alchemy. In "Shooting an Elephant," George Orwell shows how it can work. He renders a small, ugly incident of his experience with such precise detail that it becomes mythic. One day in Moulmein—less than a day, a moment. An escaped elephant. Confused information. A shooting. Just the usual work, really, in the life of a colonial police officer. But Orwell describes the shooting in painful detail—the fine elephant rifle, five deliberate shots, his miscalculated aim, the failure of his bullets, the elephant's slow tortured dying, prolonged agony, more shots (into its heart, down its throat), the labored breathing, blood, Orwell's inability to stomach the spectacle any longer, and the bystanders' flaying the elephant's body even before it has died.

In the light of Orwell's reflective imagination, the meanings condense. He hated being laughed at. His whole life as an imperial officer in Burma was devoted to trying vainly to maintain his self-respect in the face of natives who despised him and whom he had come to detest. His candor about his own meanness dismays and instructs us. The more he inquires into the particulars of his experience, the more universally significant it becomes. His delineation of petty vanity becomes an indictment of empire. He shot the elephant simply in order to save face. But it was not only his face; it was the face of the British Empire. He had become trapped by the empire he served: "I perceived in this moment that when the white man turns tyrant it is his own freedom that he destroys."

Though I will probably continue hesitating when asked whether the subject of my English 101 is creative writing, I believe it is. The course's central assignment asks students to represent their experience in a way that matters to them and that they think will be significant to others. In order to do that, they must think not only about writing but about themselves and their world. In composing a personal experience essay, they must define themselves, at least for the moment, saying who they think they are. They must enact what Paul de Man calls the "trope of autobiography": prosopopoeia. That is (in the etymology of the word), they must give themselves a face.

For all its value, however, autobiography is an ambiguous act. Orwell's essay again shows us how. When Bernard Crick, Orwell's biographer, searched the record of his posting in Burma, he was unable to verify the story of the shooting. By Crick's account, no documentary evidence and no reliable testimony exist that the events recounted in the essay ever actually took place. In giving himself a face in "Shooting an Elephant," therefore, Orwell may have created not only a story of his experience, but the experience itself.

I am not disheartened by that possibility. Surely, Orwell selected certain details of his memory and arranged them for a rhetorical effect. Certainly he used some of the facts of his life to compose a meaning. It is a masterful piece of narrative argument whatever its basis in fact. And its documentary ambiguity reminds us how close in autobiography fact and fiction always are.

I want both—fact and fiction, imagination and memory. I want students to write essays that dignify the facts of their own experience by selecting and shaping them with literary force. At the same time I recognize that telling stories of our lives fictionalizes them. I know that in writing here about my family, teachers, students, self, I am making us up. In representing myself as a person, I create myself as a character. The face we give ourselves is always a mask, the self we make in language a fiction. What I believe is that the meanings of such fiction are as close to the truth about ourselves as we can ever come.

7

Stories

Bᴿɪᴛɪѕʜ ᴡʀɪᴛᴇʀ Bᴀʀʙᴀʀᴀ Hᴀʀᴅʏ says that human beings cannot keep from telling stories. Sleeping and waking we tell ourselves and each other the stories of our days: "We mingle truths and falsehoods, not always quite knowing where one blends into the other. As we sleep we dream dreams from which we wake to remember, half-remember and almost remember, in forms that may be dislocated, dilapidated or deviant but are recognizably narrative." Stories, Hardy says, are the "autobiography we are all engaged in making and remaking, as long as we live, which we never complete, though we all know how it is going to end."

During a graduation party across the street last spring, I stood in my neighbor's kitchen drying dishes and talking with her about her son David's writing. She had recently read something he had written for one of his high school teachers. She had found it almost unintelligible, full of what she called "gunk." When she asked him why he didn't just come out and say what he meant, David told her that his teachers don't want that. They want it all gunked up, he said. They want it indirect, hidden. "*Do* they?" she asked me suddenly, looking at me intently as if I knew. "Do they want *that*?" I said no as quickly as I could, and she went on: "Well, I didn't think so. I thought they wanted kids to make sense, but David was *sure*. No doubt in his mind at all. Bullshit. The kids know it's bullshit, and they think the teachers want it anyway."

I was drying the dishes and setting them on the kitchen

table. She was putting them away. Thinking about David and David's teacher reminded me of Rhonda and me.

A student in one of my introductory composition courses, Rhonda had done some writing one day in class, open-ended writing, free, a memory trace. In it she suddenly happened on a moment from her childhood. She was rocking her little sister (the sister she never liked) in the front-porch rocker at their home in Buchanan, Virginia. Both girls were giggling gaily when the chair—and Rhonda's little sister—tipped off the porch into the yard. Everyone rushed out of the house and tried to comfort the fallen child. Even Rhonda looked concerned for her sister, asking if she was hurt, saying she was sorry it happened, patting her on the head. Soon it was clear that no real harm had been done. The chair was returned to the porch, and the girls were cautioned against rocking too close to the rail-less edge. But no one knew—not her sister, not her parents—what really happened: that she deliberately flipped her sister into the yard because she disliked her so.

When Rhonda called me over in class to ask me what she should do next, I suggested that she write more, that she go back through the incident, enlarge it, texture it, sharpen its meanings. I crouched down in the aisle next to her plastic and steel desk, balanced myself with my right hand on the edge of the desk top, and urged her to write more. What was it like to have a little sister you never liked? Why didn't you like her? What was it like to have her sitting in that chair and you rocking and hearing her squeals of delight? What was it like to be giggling so hard and then to hear yourself giggle, to be intent on rocking your sister and then to have the thought steal up on you that you could hurt her? What was it like to notice how the chair was edging slowly, almost imperceptibly, toward the side of the porch, and then to keep on rocking and laughing as it moved? I urged her to write more because already, in reading that first rush of memory, I could feel in it not only Rhonda's story but mine as well, not the story of just one moment but of her whole childhood, perhaps of her whole life.

When I heard my neighbor describe her son's guess about what his teachers wanted, I began to imagine what Rhonda must have thought. I pictured her getting back to her dorm room in Stuart Hall and trying to tell her roommate about what had happened during English. About how her teacher liked what she wrote and told her to go on writing. About how she didn't really understand what he wanted her to do. "He told me to write more," she's likely to have said, "but I don't know . . . I wrote all there was to it already. I don't know what more there is to say. I guess I could put some other gunk in, but I don't know if it'll be what he wants."

This story of Rhonda and David, of high school and Freshman English, of kitchens and classrooms, has little in the way of data. It is based on no tape-recorded conversation, no protocols, and—because I did not keep copies of Rhonda's writing— no scripts. It has no systematic analysis, no findings, no conclusion even. To ask if it is valid or reliable is to ask an impertinent question. It is just a story of a teacher trying to think about his work, remembering some, making some up, trying to sort out the puzzle of his experience. It is very hard to tell in it where memory ends and imagination begins.

In *The Prelude* (1799), Wordsworth narrates a harrowing experience made up of both memory and imagination. He tells us that once, as a young boy, he stole a boat and rowed stealthily out onto a moonlit lake. It was an act, he says, "of troubled pleasure." The night was clear and silent, the lake beautiful, but the traces of the boy's movements were everywhere—in the voices of the mountain echoes that followed his oars, in the line of moon-washed pools that stretched out behind the boat as he rowed. He felt a wonderful exhilaration in his skill, in the speed and power with which he rowed through the stillness, but all the while he trembled with fear. Then he noticed something. Behind the small ridge under which the boy had found the boat, a huge cliff was hidden. As he rowed onto the lake, the cliff gradually came more and more into view. The farther he rowed from the edge of the lake, the larger it loomed; the faster he rowed the more insistently it rose. Finally the boy shrank, turned the boat, and crept back to where he had found it moored.

Memory and imagination are inseparable in this story; fact and fiction merge. The story is *about* their merging. Though we know the cliff was solid and inanimate, it seemed alive. The boy's fears amassed themselves in it and strode after him. The story invites us to enter lyrically into that moment of troubled pleasure and to experience the imaginative animation of a vast guilt. For days after that night, Wordsworth says, he was cut off from his ordinary world.

> There was a darkness—call it solitude,
> Or blank desertion—no familiar shapes
> Of hourly objects, images of trees,
> Of sea or sky, no colors of green fields,
> But huge and mighty forms that do not live
> Like living men moved slowly through my mind
> By day, and were the trouble of my dreams.

The forms that move by day through our minds as teachers may not be huge and mighty, and they may not always be the trouble of our dreams, but they have a profound impact on our teaching. They are the stories by which, as teachers, we come to understand ourselves.

Teacher knowledge is a term by which educational researchers identify the subtle understanding that grows out of teacher practice. Our knowledge enables us to respond to the complex, specific, and dynamic demands of particular teaching situations. It combines knowledge of content, pedagogical skill, and what one researcher, Lee Shulman, calls the "wisdom of practice." As such, teacher knowledge is not abstract or generalized, but embedded in actual school experience. According to Walter Doyle, another researcher studying teacher knowledge, "what teachers know about chunks of content, instructional actions, or management strategies is tied to specific events that they have experienced in classrooms." Teacher knowledge is represented, then, in one of its most important forms in the stories we tell ourselves, fellow teachers, and students of moments of our teaching and learning, moments in which we were thrilled or troubled or surprised by the most complicated joy.

During the first class meeting one semester in Freshman English, I talked too much. I do not remember why. Usually I ask students the first day to interview and introduce each other to the rest of us, but that day I did something else, so it took me far longer than usual to learn their names. It was several weeks before I felt I had a fairly sure grasp of who was who, and even then the quietest students eluded me.

The class met in the basement of Curie, the science building, a huge black lab table at the front of the room with two sinks and a couple of gas jets. The ceiling was a maze of pipes and heating ducts. She was the quietest student. She never spoke in class. The first three class days devoted to group reading of drafts, she was absent. She sat in the second row, in the fifth desk. Even when she was present she seemed absent. Our eyes never connected. When I looked over to her, she was always looking down, writing some note or other, picking paper scraps out of her notebook spiral.

She gave me her first and third essays to read and mark. I cannot remember what they were about. The second essay she brought to my office for a conference. The fourth essay she did not submit. The rest of her record is blank. On the twelfth of October, I received a form memo from the dean, addressed to me and all her other teachers, informing us that she had withdrawn from the university. Almost our entire relationship, then, is bound up for me in that one conference in my office during which we talked about her second essay. I do not have a copy of her paper, but I remember it.

It was a letter to her grandfather who lived in northern California, a letter of thanks for the summer she had just spent with him. She was trying to explain why the visit was so important to her. Having grown up in the East, she had never seen the West Coast, never seen the gray, fog-bound Pacific. All summer she and her grandfather had lived together in his small house near the water. They had wandered along the beach, watched the weather and the shore birds, talked, permitted each other to sit alone in silence. She wanted him to know how much it had meant to her, that summer, and the feeling was practically beyond words.

She told me that she couldn't read the paper to her classmates. When she tried to read it aloud to me in my office, she was unable to make it all the way through. Coming to college had been hard for her, she said by way of explanation, far harder than she had thought it would be. But she wanted to send the letter to her grandfather. She had something to tell him that she wanted him to know. When she stopped reading, I read the rest aloud myself.

One day she was down on the beach alone. At the edge of the ocean, on a shelf of still wet sand, she came upon a dying seal. She didn't know what to do. The seal's glistening body heaved, but otherwise it did not move. Its eyes were open. She knelt down next to it and waited. All day she waited there, watching. Once, when she reached her hand out and rested it on the fur of the seal's neck, she could feel its labored breathing in her fingers. She quickly pulled her hand away. Later she found that she could caress its side without feeling that she was making its work harder, so for a while she did that. Eventually the seal's eyes closed, and before the tide came back in its panting also stopped. She still sat there for a time. When she finally rose to dig a grave for the seal, her legs were sore and locked tight, so she stumbled in her awkward work. When she was done with the burial, she smoothed the sand with her hands and left the water to do the rest.

The reason she was writing this to her grandfather was that she had not told him about it at the time. She had made up some story about her day—she didn't know why, couldn't say even now, something about how she felt, well, *responsible* for that death—and now she wanted him to know the truth.

By the end of the fourth week of the semester, she had stopped coming to class. By the end of the fifth, she was gone. Such a story reminds me that I am sometimes helpless as a teacher, that sometimes all I can do is sit by and watch. But I want to resist turning the story into a parable. If I try to say what its point is, I have to generalize the experience—her, me, the seal, the paper, and that mythic seashore where she knelt. If it can be analyzed into domains, if it can be reduced to findings or implications for research, I want to insist that it was not made to have any. It is a story, one fragment of my knowledge as a teacher.

The irony of my argument on behalf of stories is that I am making it at all. I should just use this space to tell one, but I have been afraid to. I have included some fragments—moments of memory, spots of time—but the argument has abashed me with its claim: that the stories we tell will be deeply valuable to us, that in telling them we will define ourselves and what we know, that in hearing them we will remember who we are and what teaching and learning have come to mean to us. Still, that characterization of stories does not describe their purpose so much as their effect. The purpose is the same as has always moved tellers and listeners—the pleasure of the story.

My youngest son, Stephen, is in the fifth grade. He had to do a report this year on Marco Polo, a written report and an oral presentation in front of the class. The report was due on Friday, so on Monday he rode his bike down to the public library, looked up two encyclopedia articles on Marco Polo, made photocopies of them, and brought them home. Tuesday and Wednesday he spent at the computer, typing what he titled the "1rst Draft" of his report.

We had some grief over that draft: he wanted to use the copies of the articles he had brought home (he kept calling them his "data"; "I can't write it without my data," he kept saying); but I wanted him to write it out at least once without looking at the articles, just the way he had told it to me in the car on the way home from Kmart. And by the way, I told him, when you get all done with this, remind me to read you a poem about Kubla Khan, the emperor with whom Marco lived and worked. He waved this away with an OK and went on with his complaint.

"You're making me do it *your* way," he said.

"Yes," I said. "Now get to work. I'm trying to type. You type, too."

By the time his mom called from the National Reading Conference in Tucson where she was spending the week, he was reconciled to his work. He had almost a page, he told her happily, pointing at the screen as he talked into the phone. "This is my first draft," he told her. "I'm free-minding it."

Thursday night I showed him how to do the spell check and how to double-space (his freckled face beamed when suddenly he had two pages, not one). Then we saved his file under a new name so he wouldn't lose the earlier draft.

"You mean I get to keep them both?" he asked, amazed.

When we printed out the final version, he was so excited by

it that he kept thinking of people he wanted to give copies to—
his teacher, of course, and one for himself and one for me and
one for his sister and one for his brother in California.

At breakfast Friday morning, as he was reading it aloud
over his cereal, he noticed a glitch. "That's not right," he said.
"'*On* Marco and his father go back to Venice'? *That's* not right.
It should be '*Then* Marco and his father go back.'"

Downstairs to the computer, load up the file, make the
change, save it under a new name, draft three, no time to make
extra copies now, but Stephen grabs all three versions for his
teacher and races for the school bus that's already honking at
the corner.

The report was a success, he told me Friday afternoon. He
was nervous in front of the class, and his teacher asked him to
give his presentation twice, but she said it was *excellent*, an
evaluation Stephen underlined in the air with his voice.

Then I read the poem to him.

> In Xanadu did Kubla Khan
> A stately pleasure dome decree:
> Where Alph, the sacred river, ran
> Through caverns measureless to man
> Down to a sunless sea.

I planned to give him all sorts of explanation, but at the
last moment I decided just to read. No glosses on "athwart,"
"cedarn," "momently," or "Mount Abora." Just the poem, trying to revive within us its symphony and song. When I got to
the end, Stephen said—his highest compliment—"*Cool*."

I think he meant it. As we went up the stairs from the basement to get some more stove wood, he said, "You know the
part I liked best? That part about the dome of sun and the caves
of ice. *Yeah*," he said. "That was *cool*."

8

Failure

ONE SPRING I was asked to speak at a luncheon for prospective scholarship students and their parents at Radford. The talk was well received. The audience included, along with students and parents, all the academic deans of the university, many department chairs, members of the board of directors of the University Foundation (which distributed the scholarships), the director of the university's public information office, and the executive assistant to the university president. The talk was subsequently printed in a special issue of the alumni magazine directed at prospective new students to Radford. It was a hopeful talk, the story of my work with one student in Freshman English on one paper, a story about learning and love.

The next year I was invited to speak again. I agreed, but with some tacit reluctance. As the date for the talk grew nearer, I became increasingly uneasy. I had spoken before of my experience of hope and love in teaching; now I felt neither. Though free to say whatever I liked, I could not imagine telling that audience of the dismay and sadness pervading my work. They would be hopeful; Radford University would be a promise to them on that spring afternoon. There would be flowers on the linen tablecloths in the Muse banquet room. Lunch would be delicious. I had waited too long to back out. So I searched for some way to make my sense of failure redeeming, and I talked about that.

I told them that I too had been a scholarship student. I too had earned good grades. The liability of my success (and I suggested it might be of theirs as well) was that I had grown afraid of failure. Addicted to A's, I was a student impatient for right answers. Irony unsettled me. I rarely revised; I would merely wait for the right word or phrase and write that down. But the experience of failure, I said, is good. At the very heart of our best experiences in school lies failure, and if we are too frightened to accept it, our learning will be diminished.

I believe what I said that afternoon, but I knew even then that I was not telling the whole story.

English department meetings at Radford are usually held in one or another classroom on the fourth floor of Young. We pack the place, regular faculty, temporary instructors, graduate teaching fellows, all sitting in rows like students, the aisles full of our legs, bags, coats, umbrellas.

In the middle of one meeting, a young woman stood up, her face blanched, picked her way awkwardly toward the door and out into the hall. By the time I reached her, a friend was urging her to sit down and lean against the cinder block wall, and someone else was calling the emergency squad. The meeting went on as we waited there, listening to the siren, then to the rescue team bursting through the fire door at the end of the corridor. The young woman was awake but weak and disoriented. As the medics hooked her up to their monitors and took their readings, the stretcher arrived on the elevator. I can't now explain what seems in my memory to be a long pause, but finally they eased her onto the stretcher, took her down to the ambulance, and, her friend having gotten in behind her, sped off to the community hospital.

Whatever we were waiting for during that pause, my memory is that I sat on the floor next to her, holding her head in my hands and trying, though I did not know how, to comfort her.

She had enrolled as a graduate student in the teaching fellow program which I at that time directed. Teaching two sections of Freshman English and taking two graduate courses, she was at the same time studying for a master's degree and learning to teach. The work exhausted; it seemed impossible. My advice was little help. Near the end of her first semester, she was already considering withdrawing from the program. She was not satisfied with it or the university or the town or me. She loved teaching, she told me, but in spite of that, perhaps because of it, she decided as Christmas approached to leave.

When I visited her in her apartment later that evening, home from the hospital, she was in her robe, drinking soup or tea, and she and her friend and I talked lightly about how glad we were that she was fine. But she was not fine. The experience of being a teaching fellow had incapacitated her. Our talk with one another had been fruitless. Like sitting together in the hall waiting for the rescue squad, it did not connect us at all.

As different as my many failures are in working with students, they are all in some sense like that one: we are disconnected, and I do not know what to do about it. Further, such failure haunts me, shadowing my days with grief.

I am afraid of failure. Like most college professors, I have grown accustomed to academic success. I was an A student. I attended fine schools, the last a prestigious one. My work, as both a student and a teacher, has received recognition of various kinds, scholarships and fellowships to study, prizes for writing, and, at Radford, one of the university's faculty teaching awards. In a way that is familiar to many people, my sense of myself as a person is tied closely to such success. In *Habits of the Heart*, Robert Bellah and his colleagues say that for middle-class Americans the definition of work is very close to the definition of self; "what we 'do,'" they say, "often translates to what we 'are.'" Certainly, this has been so for me.

The University of Santa Clara nominated me for a Rhodes Scholarship in 1966. When the California selection committee interviewed me at Cal Tech in Pasadena, I was an English major with a minor in Latin. First question:

"Mr. Murphy, what connections have you noticed between your studies of Latin literature and your studies of English literature?"

Connections? What? I thought as fast as I could, scanned all the memory I could reach, came back empty. No connections there. The truth was that I had not noticed any. When Fr. Kropp, my Latin teacher, said, "For next class, translate these five odes of Horace," that's what I did. When Mr. Heffernan said, "Study these poems by Alexander Pope," that's what I did. I was not making connections. I was doing homework. Sitting in that semicircle of interviewers, my mind was blank. The name I blurted out—without any sense of connection; I was thankful for a name—was Greek.

I never recovered. I stumbled and mumbled and giggled embarrassedly. With one question they had exposed me. Nothing I said to them after that carried any conviction in my ear. I felt like a cheat. It was not my knowledge of Latin and English that I found inadequate; it was myself. At the center of all my previous success was a fragile, shivering self, abject and vain.

Some years later, as a graduate student, I arranged a tutorial in the comic drama of Restoration England. At our second meeting of the term, in a cramped attic office under the sloped roof of Wheeler Hall, the professor asked me a question about the works I was to have read. I had done my homework, read the plays—by Wycherley, Etherege, Farquhar, Vanbrugh, probably at least one by Congreve. What was different, he asked, about how the later plays ended?

Simple question. I had just read them. Which were the "later" plays? I could not say. I had not thought about their dates. Ridiculous. Take a week to read four or five plays, and come to a tutorial without knowing when they were written? But even as I was pausing to discover that I did not know their chronology, the authors started to slip away from me, and then the plays themselves. Endings? How *did* they end? My teacher sat there looking at me, waiting. I panicked.

I read for the rest of the semester on my own, wrote a paper, dropped it off in his department mail box, and only went back to his office when the term was over to pick up my graded essay. At first I blamed myself, for being unprepared, for not knowing how to prepare, for mumbling, for panicking. Then I blamed him, for asking so ruinous a question. I never explained to him what had happened to me; I couldn't imagine doing so. I never wanted to talk to him again.

Only much later was I able to realize how the fear of failure had disabled me in moments like those. It was this realization that I tried to convey to the scholarship students and their parents at the luncheon: precisely because we have been successful, we are especially vulnerable to such fear. I went on to say, however, that recognizing the fear actually frees and enables us. Success in school, I argued—in reading poetry, in writing essays—actually depends on accepting failure in the process of learning.

Reading some poetry confuses, perplexes us. It confronts us with words that do not seem to mean what we expect them to mean or (perhaps for a long time) anything at all. But in our confusion, which we must accept if we want to read, we get considerable power. Take the first sentence from *Paradise Lost*:

> Of man's first disobedience, and the fruit
> Of that forbidden tree, whose mortal taste
> Brought death into the world, and all our woe, . . .
> Sing, Heav'nly Muse.

Because we do not yet know what it means, we can notice the word *first* and begin to realize that this is a poem not only about the sin of Adam and Eve in paradise, "man's first disobedience," but also about the disobedience that has continued ever since. And the word *fruit*—because the lines perplex us and thwart easy reading, that is, because in trying to read them we are likely to fail, we can linger over the word *fruit* and wonder about it and begin to realize that it refers not only to the apple on the tree of knowledge of good and evil. The "fruit / Of that forbidden tree" is also the bitter fruit of that first sin— "death"—and not only death but "all our woe," catastrophe compounding itself. In reading some poetry, we must permit ourselves to be confused. We must try not to be so afraid for ourselves that we grab onto the first meaning we can find and hang on for dear life.

When we write a draft of an essay—unless we are very lucky—we had also better be prepared for failure. Almost no one gets it right the first draft. Sometimes all the first draft is good for is to help us clear our throats. Even once that is out of the way, there is plenty of failure to be had, ignorance, clichés, lies. If we wish to revise what we have written, or for some reason must revise it, revision can easily become the territory of danger that, Peter Elbow reminds us, old mapmakers once marked "there be monsters." Revision may look more like failure than anything else, as the pieces of what we've written disintegrate and their substance dissolves. All writers fail. They tell us again and again how hard it is: blood, madness. They tell themselves. But we all forget, and every time we begin again, we have to stumble and limp through the mazes of our thought and fear.

This was a luncheon speech, however, so I framed it with a cheerful anecdote about my younger son, and a piece of his writing. The summer before, I had run in the Vashon Island Strawberry Festival 10K. The race began too late on a day when the temperatures reached the mid-nineties. I finished about 250th in a field of 300. My family was there to cheer me across the line and take my picture. As soon as I could, I found some shade and as many paper cups of water as I could hold.

Stephen was eight years old, just learning to read and write. He must have taken my weariness at the end for disappointment, though in fact I had run simply for fun and was only hot and tired, not disheartened. As he watched me standing in the shade, pouring water over my head and neck and shoulders, he must have thought he saw me dejected by failure. Months later, having devised a consolation for me in his mind, he left the following note on my desk at home in Radford:

> *from Stephen*
> This is the story of
> sterrobery festival
> at vashon island
> in the festival
> you bidin't come in
> last you came in first
> in your heart.

The wisdom of his note startled and pleased me. When I read it to the audience, it pleased them too. Stephen was writing about failure and heart. "Coming in first" wasn't exactly the point I wanted, but it was upbeat, so I took his words for my theme. Accept failure, I told them; recognize its value in lives distinguished by success.

It was a misleading speech. Only between the lines could the members of that audience have read my state of mind. I am talking about us both, I told them, teachers and students. School is not a place where teachers already know what all the first lines of all the poems mean or where they have learned to write without pain. Teachers have not put confusion and ignorance behind them. Still, I sounded clear and knowing. I told stories of past failure from which I had recovered or grown. I took obvious pleasure in my son's kindness and insight. What I did not acknowledge (I could not admit it, I was sure, under the circumstances) was the aridity of my work and the fear I felt having to speak to them at all. What I did not say was that accepting failure means more than accepting it for the time being. It means entering into it, fear and all, allowing for the very real possibility that it will swallow you up.

I learned the metaphor of entering from the modern Japanese martial art of aikido. *Irimi-nage* is aikido's basic form, the movement of going in. The name *aikido* itself means "the way of breath and harmony." One joins one's partner's force, blending with it, absorbing it into a new harmony. Entering in aikido, however, is literal, not metaphorical. The heritage of the art is ancient and martial. The force one joins is destructive, maybe deadly. Entering is a matter of life and death.

In practice, the situation is formalized into a routine. Its first moment looks like this. In response to a stylized punch or kick or grab by one's partner, one steps forward, just off the line of attack but very close to it, and turns to look in the same direction as the partner, feet and legs parallel, hips oriented similarly, one's hand on the back of the partner's neck. At full speed, the frame cannot be frozen here. Both aikidoists blur into a spiral of motion that resolves itself as the partner is mysteriously thrown through the air. But films of the founder of aikido, Morihei Ueshiba, or videotapes of some of his famous students, can be paused and the moment of blending studied. The movement is astonishingly simple: rotate hips, slide forward.

My teacher, Bruce Klickstein, arranged an exercise to help us work on just that much. He would stand in the center of the practice mat and invite each of his students, one at a time, to step up and face him. Both stood still, the student waiting for the teacher to initiate his attack. Bruce's face was expressionless, his eyes unfixed. In his hands, he held a thin, hollow plastic mailing tube, about four feet long, the practice version of a sword. When he raised it and struck—in a perfectly straight line on the student's head—the mailing tube marked the line a sword would cut. If we didn't move properly, the tube would hit us. No matter; it was only plastic. But in order to make the point clear, Bruce would strike suddenly, with furious speed, his movement exploding out of stillness, and he would accompany the blow with a fierce shout, the concentrating breath (*ki*) of aikido. It was only practice, but it was deeply unnerving. I jumped, dodged to the side, stepped back, stood dumbly in place, let the tube bounce off my head. In the face of his assault, I found the simplest movement—rotate hips, slide forward—exceedingly difficult. But its difficulty is not surprising. *Irimi-nage* is an astonishing act: in a frightening situation, instead of denying or hiding, blocking or resisting, the aikidoist enters.

I have not become proficient at aikido, though twice, for years at a time, I practiced it diligently. One time, when I had returned to study with him, Bruce Klickstein told me that it felt as if I had been doing aikido in my dreams. I think he was right. Certainly I have used aikido again and again to help me think about my life as a teacher, as a person, appropriating its art—especially its distinctive entering—as a metaphor for my experience.

After my qualifying examination for the doctorate at Berkeley, I worked independently for nearly half a year on ideas for a dissertation on comedy. I gathered together a wide range of materials—the *Iliad*, Flannery O'Connor's short story "Parker's Back," a variety of trickster myths, Swift's "Tale of a Tub," *The Man of Mode*, Faulkner's "The Bear," and *Ulysses*. With a fine-tipped Rapidograph pen, I wrote pages and pages of discussion in minute black script on yellow paper. Then, because I sensed that I ought to get some interim approval for what I was doing, I wrote a brief summary of where I was and met with Ralph Rader, the teacher who had agreed to direct my dissertation.

"This won't do," he said, as kindly, as gently as he could, but without mincing words. We were sitting in the sun on the steps of California Hall, eating bag lunches, the yellow pages of my work on comedy furling in the breeze. I had no thesis yet,

Rader explained. The writing I had been eking out over the months had no bearing that he could discern, no center. What had moved me as it took inchoate shape in my mind seemed scattered to him on the page and unlikely—at least as I had summarized it to him—ever to achieve coherence or point. His reaction immediately confirmed all the secret uncertainty I had felt while I worked alone. It eliminated whatever secret hope I had permitted myself to feel. I did not resent his comments; in fact I agreed with them, though they made the work I had been doing seem wasted. More than anything I felt lost: I did not know where I was or what to do. I thanked him for his time, said I understood his criticism, and left.

I decided that night to quit the program. The next afternoon I went to talk with Rader in his office to tell him why. As difficult as it was to acknowledge, I confessed that I didn't know how to write a dissertation or how to find or construct a thesis. I had managed to get this far successfully, but faced with the principal task of the doctoral program—an extended piece of independent, professional literary scholarship—I realized that I was not capable of doing it. The most sensible course seemed to be to withdraw.

"I wouldn't do that if I were you," Rader said.

In the end, I took his advice. He helped me work through my confusion and develop a thesis I could and did write. What I want to emphasize here, however, is the experience of feeling utterly directionless, without moorings or coordinates, and of having to face that fact. In retrospect, I see that facing it turned out to be useful: Rader needed to know how disoriented I felt in order to be able to give me helpful direction. But freeze the frame as I approached the door of his office that afternoon: the only thing I feel is nausea, and the only thing I can think to do is admit it.

In the spring of 1977, I had never taught in a community college. The department chair at Alameda asked me some what-would-you-do-if questions, then leaned forward, folded his hands on the papers on his desk, and said, "I don't think you're what we're looking for. You're . . . how can I put it? . . . too diffident."

Again, it was afternoon. He hadn't turned on the overhead

light in his office. I looked out though the slot of the floor-to-ceiling window, over the parking lot and the playing field, over the rooftops of downtown Oakland and into the hills.

"We need somebody with more vitality," he said. "Our students don't respond very well to teachers who are aloof. They aren't very patient with pedants. We need somebody with spirit, with enthusiasm. And from what I can see of you . . ."

"But that's *just* what I'm good at," I said emphatically, interrupting. "I'm very resourceful. The classroom is where I do my best work. That's what students say; that's what my supervisors say. I teach my heart out." The job was slipping away. I had nothing to lose by arguing.

"OK," he said, and hired me.

Most of the first class went fine, but about two-thirds of the way through, I began to notice my own voice—pitched high as usual and resonant, but today especially thin, and racing for some reason. I began to watch myself at the front of the room, introducing the work of the course. My body was thin. One hand held the syllabus from which I read; the other moved around, looking for a place to rest, my pocket, belt, hip, the other corner of the syllabus. I woke in the middle of the night to the chairman's words about diffidence and to the purported impatience of the students. It was true; I had seen myself, static and mechanical, at the front of the classroom. Many of the students were older than I was. They were here on their lunch hour or were carrying a full load of courses on top of a night job. Their faces looked first open, then impassive, then skeptical. The room was crowded. The course was always overenrolled, I was told, with the expectation that as students dropped out, a more manageable class size would gradually be reached. I imagined that the students had given me one day of grace, but that on the second they would start to drop. Their faces would begin with skepticism, I supposed, then move to annoyance and anger. As they slammed their books and notebooks together and rose to leave in the middle of class, I could hear them muttering to each other, laughing bitterly, taking one last look at me, and saying, "What is this shit?"

In fact, as I remember it now, almost the entire second meeting was devoted to reviewing some grammar exercises I had assigned for homework from a book called *English Fundamentals*. I asked students to share the answers they had come up with and to explain how they had arrived at them. I laughed with them when they caught themselves in an error. I pointed at them with the book, apologizing because I did not yet know their names, and waved both arms to cheer their success in analyzing a run of sentences. I stepped with my whole body into an imaginary circle, rotating one way then another, to physically represent the way in which English grammar is a product of both function and form.

I never told them, however, about my fearsome images of them in the night. Nor of the hours I spent preparing that second class, shaping and reshaping its parts, writing out every sentence I planned to say. Before class, I sat in my Volkswagen along the side of the road into Alameda and reconsidered everything yet again. Then, because there was no more time and because, qualified or not, there was nothing else I could think to do, I went in to teach.

When my family moved to Radford, Christine was beginning first grade. She asked me to take her to school, as I had driven her older brother Kevin every morning for years in California. I told her I couldn't. The public school day did not begin until eight forty-five. If I drove her, I could not be at my office until nine. Too late, I thought. In before eight, home at five-thirty, back to the office after dinner to read *Paradise Lost* and plan class and grade papers. Four classes, two sections of English 101, two of the introductory course in literature, the standard college English teaching assignment in America. I became faculty sponsor of the junior class, coadvisor of the yearbook, a member of the executive board of the Virginia Association of Teachers of English, one of Radford's representatives to a consortium of state colleges interested in developing writing-across-the-curriculum programs. I laughed—like a kid working a summer job—ran from class to meetings to lectures to events. Greeted people I did not know. Chatted and joked with the housekeeping staff who emptied my wastebaskets and changed my office lights. One of my new colleagues, biologist Jack Clark, waved at me from the walk beside Reed Hall, hollered, "I hear you're doing *good* work, Rich." Linda Killen, another member of the faculty, said, "What *is* it? You are *so* cheerful. Doesn't *anything* bother you?" When I passed historian Margaret Woodhouse on the Young Hall stairs, she said, "You young people have such energy." I waved to her and laughed and raced on up the stairs, two, three at a time. One night the first winter, on my way back to school in the rain, the windshield wipers began a raucous scraping. Then the images through the glass melted, the fuzzy blades scratching the surface of the blur. It was a warning: the streets were coating with ice. I asked a colleague the next day, "How do you drive through this stuff?"

"Very cautiously," he said.

I did not know how to be cautious.

I had rigged up a worktable in the root cellar; when I worked at home this was where I holed up, poring over the fourth edition of the *Norton Anthology*, word for word, footnotes and all, trying to get ready for tomorrow's class. One Sunday afternoon, on the steps of our basement, Susie's loneliness finally grew bad enough to speak.

"If you want to work without stopping," she said quietly, "why don't you get an apartment of your own?"

She had resigned a ten-year career as a successful elementary school teacher in Oakland to permit me to take the job in Radford. Now, as she was devoting days and nights to trying to make a home for us in this unfamiliar town, I was spending as many hours as I could at work. A banal story without the banality; this time it was ours. Susie's question seemed less criticism than plea, but I knew its gravity. She had never said such a thing before. The whole structure of our life together shuddered. Anything was now possible. How deep did the failure go? Neither of us knew. I left my book in the root cellar and sat down with her on the stairs. As we talked, the bitter winter wind pressed against the basement window just above our heads.

Years later, I was working almost exclusively with graduate teaching fellows, supervising their teaching of Freshman English. A number of them had grown very dissatisfied with the program and with my direction of it. Every meeting with them seemed to me to be charged with the potential of increased frustration or ill will. The course I conducted for them in the teaching of writing was unsatisfying to us both. Some of them regarded the journal and paper I asked them to write and the books I asked them to read as unduly burdensome. I regarded their unwillingness to enter into the spirit of the work as refractory and in some cases irresponsible. My praise of individuals' writing or teaching was discounted as untrustworthy, and my criticism was resented as unfair. It was a standoff. One of the graduate teaching fellows, Jill Kazmierczak, later described the experience as like being in two camps. "It was us against him," she wrote.

Though normally I kept my door open, by the end of that year it was closed. The experience of working with those students paralyzed me. I don't doubt that I was responsible for my share of that year's failure. I believe now that my sense of their alienation stiffened me, made me less adaptive or resilient, led me to say things that only alienated them further. No attempt at resolving our differences seemed to work. One student grew suddenly ill. I arranged that she be allowed to remain in the program and assured her that she need not worry either about her classes (which would be taught in her absence) or her missed work (which could be made up later). The accommodation did not allay her distrust of me, a distrust she later told me she could neither explain nor remove. One student, overwhelmed by obligations, came frequently to my office for advice. Late one evening, called at home to come to her office, I talked with her at length, trying to encourage her to take even the difficulty of her work positively. I later learned that she regarded the advice I gave her as utterly useless and the presumption with which I gave it patronizing.

The woman on the floor in Young Hall undergoing an emergency electrocardiogram was one of the students in that group. I never reached her. She and her friend left the program at Christmas. The rest of us finished the year in a state of strained civility. One interpretation I later heard of the failure of my relationship with those students was that I would not relent, that I would not listen, that I would not understand them. I think now that there is some truth to that view. But as the year was coming to its end, I was drawn as if by vertigo to step back into the failure. I asked Jill Kazmierczak—the student who throughout the year had seemed most keenly critical, the student who when she began the program was awarded the department's one scholarship for graduate study—to tell me what had happened. I asked her to tell me what we had done to one another, to tell me how I had failed.

I told the scholarship students and their parents that failure is good, that accepting it helps us learn, that entering into it permits us to grow. I believe that. But I did not tell them the whole story. I left my fear unsaid. I did not tell them about the moments in which I have felt so lost I did not know where to turn. I said nothing about the anger or contempt I sometimes feel for students or teachers at what I regard as their laziness or indifference. Through my success run lines of vanity and habit, ambition and weariness, like gristle in the tissue of my days; these I did not trace. I did not say that for all the rush of my work, I often felt that I was accomplishing nothing, or that at the end of many semesters I could not be confident that I had taught anyone anything. It did not seem right to tell them, at the end of the scholarship luncheon, that I sent off orders for books I did not read and that the principal stuff of my reading had become magazine articles I piled to look at later and book reviews I skimmed.

I should have declined the invitation to speak, even after accepting it. But that did not seem possible. I looked around for something to say that might be appropriate to the occasion, and in the success of the scholarship students and my own sense of failure I supposed I had found it. My subject was failure. The talk was well received. I don't know if anyone there ever knew how much it belied the emptiness of my heart.

9

Grade Appeal

SOME YEARS AGO a student contested the grade he had received in Freshman English. He followed the course of action prescribed for him in the university's student handbook. First, he contacted the professor of the course and expressed his disagreement. He deserved an A, he claimed, not a B, and asked for reconsideration of his grade. When the teacher obliged, recomputed the student's average, and came up with the same grade as before, the student wrote to the department chairman. After reviewing the circumstances of the case and deciding that there was merit on both sides, the chairman forwarded it to a committee of department faculty for their consideration. They too decided that the facts of the case warranted a hearing. Student and professor were both invited to a meeting to explain their respective positions. The committee then deliberated, found in favor of the student, and asked the university registrar to change the grade to an A.

Formal grade appeals are relatively rare. More often, student dissatisfaction with grades is expressed in private vituperation of the teacher or simply absorbed as part of the unhappy experience of school. Students are deterred from more formal appeals, I think, by the procedures themselves. At Radford University, they must prepare careful documentation of their position. They must confront their teachers directly and then expose themselves and their work to the department chairpersons and ultimately a committee of faculty who, in the presence of their teachers, are sitting in judgment of them and their claim. Those are daunting requirements, compounded by the fact that they must be met during the semester following receipt of the disputed grade, while the student is enrolled in all new courses and preoccupied with the obligations set by new teachers. Add, too, the fact that student complaints about grades are very rarely sustained. Grade appeals are not publicized, but in all the years I have been at Radford, only one case I know of has been decided in favor of the student: this one. The odds of a formal appeal being worth the trouble, then, are very small. Only exceptionally adamant students with a sense of having been egregiously mistreated are likely to press such a formal complaint.

In this case, the student was especially forceful. Though he was only a freshman, and in spite of the fact that he had transferred to another university in the meantime, he carried the appeal to the end. He wrote a strong case for himself, sober and reasonable. He traveled back to Radford to appear at the hearing and there made an impressive presentation of his position. I do not know him personally, but the committee's decision in his favor surely must have been keenly satisfying to him. It not only vindicated his opinion of the grade he deserved in the course. It affirmed the stubborn insistence with which he challenged his teacher's opinion.

I know this story because the teacher was Nancy Harman, one of the graduate teaching fellows I supervised. She told me then and has told me since that it was a very difficult experience for her. Not only was she unfamiliar with the grade appeal process, she was new to teaching and uncertain about both her grading procedures and her authority as a teacher and evaluator. Her uncertainty was compounded by the fact that, as an A student herself, she had a high regard for grades. She also was keenly sensitive to the desire of students to be treated fairly by their teachers. She would have certainly been sympathetic to this student's contesting another teacher's grade, but his appeal of *hers* seemed personally hostile. Further, she was still a graduate student at the time in our department. She could not help but feel that her ultimately unsuccessful defense of herself to her professors on the hearing committee undermined her already tenuous status as a teacher. I tried to reassure her that I had confidence in her judgment and fairness. But nothing I said allayed any of her worry or could reduce any of her feeling of vulnerability. A student was appealing his grade, and he and everyone else, the whole university it seemed, were going to go over Nancy's teaching inch by inch looking for a mistake. As her supervisor, I am implicated in Nancy's story, too. She was the official instructor in the course. Her grades were her own. Still, it was her first semester teaching. If I had been more available to her or supervised her grading more closely, perhaps she might have been able to avoid the conflict she became embroiled in. I helped her through the process of the appeal, but it was she who suffered. If I had helped her earlier, I tell myself, maybe her suffering would have been unnecessary.

At the same time, I know that grading is always fraught with difficulty. As particular as Nancy's story is, it embodies for me some of the more general problems of grading that vex our work in school. The grade appeal formalizes the relationship in which teachers and students are finally alienated from each other.

I remember first hearing of the situation over the phone: Nancy's voice, strained with panic. A student was appealing his grade. She needed to respond. What should she say?

"I don't know," I said. "Tell me what happened."

Nancy wanted to give grades in her course. As a student, she had wanted to receive them. They had caused her some agony, driving her as they did each semester, but at the same time she had thrived with them. Teaching or attending school without grades was inconceivable. So when I described my own practice at the time of not grading individual assignments in Freshman English, it simply baffled her. I can understand why.

Grades were my compass in school as a student. They helped me see where I was and where I was going. I can't remember being given a single ungraded assignment, and I am reasonably sure I would have felt such a project incomplete, trivial even, for lacking a grade. I know that if I had been set such a task at the same time as a graded one, I would have devoted my best energy and concentration to the assignment with the grade. One of the most surprising difficulties I encountered when I began teaching full time was the negative consequence of being finally free of grades. I discovered I wanted a report card. I wanted to be graded on how I was doing. Still today, I ask students for evaluations of my work every term. Because of my rank and tenure, that frequent a review is no longer required by the university, but I continue to ask for it anyway, partly because of the appeal grades still have to me.

Nevertheless, I began not giving grades on individual assignments in Freshman English. For a long while I shied away from the practice even though I had read about it in the professional literature of composition teachers. Then, as part of a study conducted with a colleague, I wanted to watch how students would write and revise their essays if there were no grade either to motivate the writing or to provide an external mark to end the process. I did not grade surreptitiously and keep the grades in a secret ledger. I simply did not determine a grade for individual pieces of writing at all.

That approach to evaluation immediately seemed more consistent with the kind of work I was asking students to do. It allowed them to write numerous drafts without having to correct each as they went along. It permitted false starts and the chance to work further on a paper that had earlier been abandoned. It gave students a greater degree of authority over the schedule, progress, and finish of any particular piece of writing. They could say when they considered it complete or when they had decided to stop working on it. Without the prospect of an immediate grade, students tended to be more willing to address someone other than the teacher as the intended audience of their work. Further, my verbal responses (since they were irreducible to a grade) were more likely to strike students as the opinions of a reader or editor, that is, as someone concerned with the writing as writing, than as the disguised verdict of a judge. The approach helped me, too. It permitted me to be more positive, in both praise and criticism of a student's work. It allowed me to focus on the achievements of the writing without having to weigh them against the failures. It also made it possible for me to frame my editorial advice as options to consider rather than as instructions to follow for correctly completing the assignment.

"But how does it work?" Nancy and other graduate teaching fellows wanted to know. "If you don't grade the papers, how can you tell how the students are doing? How can *they* know?"

The students wondered the same thing. Enrolling in my course, many students found themselves floating in a bottomless sea. I said, "If you want to know how you are doing in the course, come and see me. We'll talk about it, review your work, and I'll give you a grade for the course as of that date." Almost no one came.

Some said, "I didn't want to know but, not knowing, I was scared to death."

At the end of a conference in my office with one student, I asked, "Would you like to talk about your grade?"

"No," he said. "I don't need to know." Then, in his course evaluation, he wrote that he considered the grading system very unfair: "I never knew where I stood."

One student went home for an early semester weekend, told his father about not receiving grades on his papers. "Sounds fishy," his father said. "Better watch out for that guy." Then at the end of the term—when we were meeting in a final conference about his semester grade—he told me what his father had said.

"I should've listened to him," the student declared. "You did just what he said you would—you dicked me over."

Nancy wanted none of that. Even if the benefits I outlined seemed desirable, such potential negative effects made her decisive. Not only did she want to avoid conflict with students; she thought the students were right. They deserved to know their grades. Evaluating without grading seemed vaguely dishonest to her, and holistic grading at the end of the semester seemed something like a magic trick. Far better to grade every paper and compute the grades. Such an approach is not only clearer but fairer. It allows student energy to be devoted to the work rather than absorbed by persistent worry about the final grade.

But whatever grading system a teacher uses, many students *will* worry. As long as their work will be graded sometime, now or later, they are helplessly preoccupied with what they will get. Two young women walking down the hall on the fourth floor of Young have come to retrieve their papers from a cardboard box outside their teacher's office. They wait until they start down the stairs before looking. "Ooh . . . ," says one, shivering, as they pass my open door. "I'm so scared."

At the beginning of a class meeting in one of my courses, a student couldn't contain himself. He swung the desk in front of him around, put his feet up on the chair, leaned back, picked up his book bag, dropped it again on the floor, sat up straight. "I'm sorry," he said finally. "I'll be all right in a minute." But he continued to fidget and sigh.

"What's the matter?" I asked.

"Nothing. I just got my Shakespeare paper back."

The rest of the students were subdued. I discovered later that many of them were in the same course with him, that they had just come from Shakespeare. A set of papers had been returned. They all got A's or B's on their papers; he got a D. They were unable to imagine why they succeeded where he failed. They sympathized with him, but they didn't want him to know how well they had done.

I asked freshmen one semester to record in journals their different experiences in the course. Here is what one wrote as she waited for me to return her graded essay:

> What's my paper's grade? I don't know, he is going to get it now. I wonder what he wrote. I probably got a F because of my punctuation. God! Please don't let me get a D+ or lower, anything else, give me anything else, a C- please, he handed it to me so slowly. He knows it Bad. He hates it. He failed me. I'll look now.

Another student in the same class wrote this in response to the grade he had just received:

> I got a fucking D, that's swell just what I needed in this stupid mother-fucking course. I hate writing this fucking shit.

Such fear and anger startle me. In the ordinary course of my daily work, I forget them. I imagine that students can have their eyes and hearts fixed on what they are writing. "Forget the grade," I say airily; "concentrate on the meaning you are trying to compose." Or I admit their absorption with grades and protest that they have nothing to fear. They have lucked out; they have a fair, honorable teacher: me. But all my attempts to downplay the grades I put on student essays leave some students thinking, "Oh, God! Please . . ." or "Swell, a fucking D." I forget: I was myself absorbed by grades. My not noticing the play of student fear or anger is as foolish as anything else I can think of in my life as a teacher.

All grading systems are flawed, including the one I proposed to Nancy and the other graduate teaching fellows the year she began to teach, including the one she finally settled on for herself. I have since turned to yet another system. Now I give students a choice: they may have all their assignments graded individually, or only some of them, or none. Still, this alternative merely diffuses the problems; it does not solve them. Much of the time, grades interfere with the work of both teachers and students in school. Sometimes, they pervert it.

In a writing course one recent spring semester, Christy Howard said, "The bottom line is this: the teacher is giving out the grades." Everyone knew she had spoken the truth.

"The teacher says he loves the poetry in *A Midsummer Night's Dream*," she went on. "So guess what percentage of the class loves the poetry in *A Midsummer Night's Dream*? What we're learning is to lie."

Asked to write an essay in Freshman English about a personal experience that frightened her, Christy had described a day she spent jumping off cliffs at a mountain lake:

> I turned the paper in, and the next class received it back with a note at the bottom. "I need to speak to you about your paper." The teacher told me that I had not expressed my fear well enough. I didn't understand. "You need to make your experience even more frightening," said Miss Smith. "But this is how it happened," I said. Then the inevitable one sentence. "Well, unless you change it, it is just not that interesting." Well, there you go. I took the paper home, added a few *fictitious* moments and got an "A." "I love your revision," Miss Smith said. I lied about an event in my life to get the grade.

The class was shocked by Christy's candor, then cheered. It was like a revival meeting. Other students seconded her stories, nodding, calling out their agreement. One student tried in vain to stop it: "You guys," she pleaded, leaning out over her desk with her arms outstretched, "don't . . . don't let him hear our secrets." One student told me later: "That was it—what Christy said—that was the truth. All my years in school I've wanted to say that and never had the guts."

I was glad to hear it, too, glad it was being aired. I thought the moment presented an opportunity for me to make an appeal of my own.

"This is wonderful," I said, "this admission. You know what it means? It means that since you understand what is happening to you, you can stop it. You can refuse to lie. You can reject the seduction of the grade . . ."

They looked at me. Then they laughed.

For hours, Nancy and I sat together at Hardee's going over the draft of her letter to the hearing committee. She brought ten pages of writing, trying to tell the whole of her story.

"Explain to me again how you worked out this student's grade," I asked. I knew that the committee would need to understand what she did in order to make a decision. In spite of all she had written, I was having trouble following it.

Her account was a rush of numbers. Imagine paragraphs filled with computations, with scratched-out figures, all linked by emphatic assertions that expressed assurance but sounded frantic. Nancy had been near the end of her first semester of teaching, doing her first set of final grades. She wanted more than anything to do it right. It seemed to me that that was why she insisted on replaying the calculations. If she could show that her arithmetic was correct, then the grade she gave the student should have been the right one.

Shouldn't it?

The figures blurred for me as I listened.

My grade book is full of computing. This morning, for instance, I looked at my records for English 72, a writing course I taught at Santa Clara in 1978. For each of the six essays, I wrote down a letter grade, then translated it into a number, added up the numbers, averaged them, and translated the result back into a letter. On the two pages devoted to the general introductory course in British literature, spring semester 1984, I attached a note to myself with a paper clip that has since rusted.

I was double-checking Jennifer's grade: she got an F on the midterm, a low D on the first paper, a B- on the second, and a C- on the final. On a scale of 4.0, I averaged her grades together as 1.2, then translated that number into a course grade of D+. If anyone wants to know why a student in those courses received a certain grade—though I may have forgotten both her and her work completely—I can point to such numbers years later and say.

The lure of numbers is seductive. The whole institutional machinery of transcripts and grade-point averages in school depends on them. Their precision and dependability are so appealing that only quantitative grading seems responsible. Yet all my meticulous numerical records, measuring and calculating the performance of students, feel at once reassuring and fraudulent. When I grade a student paper, journal, class presentation, or essay exam, then translate that grade into a number and compute the numbers of all the same student's work for the course, I appear to be doing something objective and precise. But the entire process depends on a set of personal judgments that are subjective and impressionistic. Numbers mask the irreducibly personal elements of my judgment. Even when the arithmetic is correct, as it was in Nancy's case, the numbers can come out wrong.

Near the end of the semester, Nancy had taken hours to project all the students' course grades. The results perplexed and worried her. She noticed that many were higher than she believed they should be. One belonged to the student who later appealed. She hadn't imagined that such a result would be possible. If the grades on his earlier work were accurate, then the final grade should be so too. Yet his course work, taken as a whole, didn't seem characterized by the kind of excellence she associated with an A. Nancy filled scratch sheets with numbers, trying to work around the problem. The solution she came up with was to set the final values of grades and numbers so that A+ was equivalent to 98, A to 95, A- to 92, B+ to 88, and so on. She applied the scale uniformly to the work of all students in the course. It had the virtue of allowing her to compute the letter grades together and of producing the semester grades she thought all the students' work deserved. It had the disadvantage of looking as if she were arbitrarily manipulating numbers.

"What sort of scale is this?" the student asked her when she explained to him in conference that he would get a B for the course. He had a 91-point-something average—they agreed about that—just a fraction of a point below Nancy's cutoff for an A. Arguing from his experience in other courses, the student insisted that Nancy should have used what he called a ten-point scale. If she had, 90 would have been equivalent to an A- and, because Radford does not record plusses and minuses on transcripts, he would have received an A for the course.

In the appeal hearing, he made this argument again. Nancy remembers several faculty seconding it. "If 98 is an A+," one member of the committee asked, "then what's 100?" She wasn't actually using a scale, they implied (and apparently in the end concluded), but was simply trying to find a way to mark the student down.

In effect, she was caught in the snare of her own calculations. If she had given no grades numerical value, it would have been impossible to say what the student's average would have been. The question would have had no meaning. Letters cannot be averaged. On the other hand, the question of what his course grade would have been *could* be answered. When Nancy reviewed his finished essays, she found most of them reasonably good, but one only barely satisfactory. His revisions were generally substantial and thoughtful, and one was excellent. He had also done good work in his journal and in helping other students in reading and in responding to their papers. Based on all of those considerations, and comparing his work to the work of other students in the course ("He was unquestionably a good student," Nancy says, "but his work was not nearly so consistently strong as that of several other students")—she judged that his course work deserved a B.

"They weren't there," she now says, referring to the hearing committee. "They didn't see his papers or his revisions. They weren't with him in conference. All they saw were the grades."

In fact, no one disputed her judgment. The student didn't appeal on the ground that his work was really excellent and thus deserving of an A. The committee that heard the appeal did not find fault with Nancy's judgment either. They were willing to concede that she had accurately assessed the quality of the student's performance in the course. Everyone was concerned with what she did with those numbers.

"OK," I said to her over the table at Hardee's, "let's assume your calculations are right. What I want to get clear is where he got the idea that 90 should be an A?"

She had included no numerical scale in her course description. She had not announced any scale in class.

"He just assumed it," she said. No one saw the scale until the final conferences. Nancy had only just worked it out herself.

"He was shocked to discover that the cutoff for an A was 92. He came back several times that week, interrupting my conferences with other students, to talk more about it. He kept saying it was unfair. But," she added plaintively, amazed in her turn at the situation she found herself in, "wasn't I right? It was the grade he deserved."

He thought she had tricked him. He was angry. He would not accept her explanation or her rationale. But she never thought he would appeal. When he did, she was ashamed and angered. He was turning school into court. She was being sued. On the phone, at the lunch table, over drafts of her letter, in her voice and eyes was always this: their disagreement over his grade had grown into alienation. In the juridical process, they had become enemies. What began as a collaborative teaching and learning relationship was now little more than a bitter personal conflict.

I understand such feelings. Their seeds lie in my everyday work. On the day I return graded tests or papers to students in class, I always plan carefully how to do it. When should I hand them back, for example—at the beginning of class, at the end? Students say, "Do you have our papers graded?" If I say yes, or if they see me walk in with the stack under my arm, they are anxious to have them returned immediately. I think it is better to wait until class is nearly over, but it probably does not matter. Either way—looking at a graded paper and thinking about it or anticipating the grade on a paper soon to be returned—student concentration on such days is hopelessly divided.

I am distracted too. I think about how to give the papers back. Walking around the room and personally returning them to individual students? Standing by the door and calling out names and distributing the papers one by one? Placing them on my desk and then getting out of the way as students rummage for their work? The desk is quickly surrounded, the pile of papers scattered as the first students sort through it. A young man in a blue polo shirt, book bag over his right shoulder, picks his essay up gingerly by the staple. As he turns his body sideways to slip back out through the crowd, he lifts the paper up above the heads of those nearby, the white pages fluttering. Since I am standing by the windows, the crowd blocks my view of the classroom door. "What did you get? What did you get?" someone asks. I cannot hear the answer.

I try to plan what to say as I return student work—nothing? a personal remark to particular individuals? some general comments about how "you" did, as if the whole class were a single person whose performance could somehow be uniformly described? public highlighting of some distinguished successes or instructive failures? I remember sitting through such general commentary by my teachers. It was never helpful to me. I was always waiting for my paper, waiting for my grade. I had little interest in success or failure not my own, wanted the teacher to stop talking and just hand the papers back.

Whatever class work I have prepared, our minds are divided. If I haven't given back the papers yet, I know what the students don't: their grades. If I've already returned them, they know what I don't: their reaction to those grades. We are looking at each other, perhaps even talking to each other, pretending to do something like discuss, lecture, take notes, question, analyze. But in fact we are both obsessed by something else.

I am not alone in this. A teacher I know tells me a story. She put a stack of graded papers to be returned to her class on the front desk at the end of the hour. As the rest of the students converged on the pile, one bypassed the graded papers and approached her to talk. The teacher could barely listen, fixed as

113

she was by the sight of hands reaching, groping, clutching for those papers. As she tells the story, her own hands mimic theirs. Her back was to the chalkboard. She was talking with a student. But she couldn't take her mind off the hands. The next day, the same student called to set up an appointment. "I'm sorry," she said, "I know this is awful. But I need to ask you to explain again what you were saying yesterday afternoon. I just couldn't concentrate on our talk. I kept thinking about the grade I would get on my paper. I tried to listen, but I couldn't."

Student and teacher both, apparently working together, distracted, alienated from one another by grades.

In those semesters when I grade holistically, I can feel the withdrawal occur. Somewhere around the tenth week or so, I start thinking about grades, start talking about them over lunch with colleagues. Like pain slipping through the last of the anesthetic, it creeps over me. I find myself more annoyed by absences from class. I notice that some students are still not bringing complete drafts of their essays to discuss. The talk in class flags. I let it and notice that some students never seem to have anything to contribute to the group conversation. Earlier a student said she intended to revise one of her essays. I notice that she hasn't done so yet. Sharon comes by class to drop off a paper, then run.

"Where are you going?" I say. "It's class time."

"I know. Gotta go," she says. "My ride to Washington's leaving at eleven. Gotta do my hair before then." And she's off down the hall.

Early in the semester, I would have stopped her, laughed, said something like "Sharon, Sharon, we need you here; you need us. Do your hair later." Now I let her go.

I turn back into the room and think, "Does this girl know how lousy her work is? Does she realize she's in danger of flunking this course?"

Distance.

I think the students and I are not working together as we used to; then I realize that I am the one changing. I am molting, turning into a judge, marking what is limited, missing, failed. What I regarded as unlimited possibility at the beginning of the semester seems to me now to have fixed itself in a small space. When I recognize what is happening—that I am getting ready to grade—I try to see the positive, the accomplishment, the good in student work. But even *that* I am distant from, scrutinizing it for evaluation rather than celebrating it, combining it with other pieces that are more ragged. In such light, even the good loses some of its lustre.

I do not withdraw *in order to* grade; the distance is in the act itself. Grading alters my relationship to students and to their work. The same writing I fostered two months earlier with hope and cheer I finally have to admit will not be completed by the end of the semester. The student I earlier admired for his astute self-criticism I must finally agree with: he does procrastinate; he doubts his own ideas so severely that he keeps himself from writing them down; what he does get written is so strained and thin that it bears almost no relation to the passionate impulse that sparked it. I loved talking with him. I do not want the semester to end. But his work? Only marginally adequate. When I deliver that judgment—to him or to the registrar or to myself—I realize that our relationship is fundamentally changed. And damaged.

I wake up worrying about the grades I give. Whether I grade every paper individually or the work of the course as a whole, I always feel (at least about some students) wrong. I graded them too high, too low, misjudged them in relation to other students in the same class. But if I am honest with myself, I admit that my worry is not only that I am unfair. It is that the students will not agree with the grade I give. Not that they will appeal it (like Nancy, I don't imagine it will go so far), but that they will dismiss it. And me. That the working relationship of trust and respect we have developed over months will dissolve in their criticism of my grading.

"Can I come by and discuss my grade?" they ask. "Can I talk with you about my paper? Can I see my final?"

Harmless questions, but I shiver when I hear them. If I were wired to a polygraph machine, the stylus would fly off the page. I am afraid of this talk, afraid I have made a mistake, afraid I have been insincere, afraid that—even if my judgment has been expert—they will regard it as wrong or inept. I do not let on. I keep my uncertainty to myself. We are not working together any more.

Such private feelings are never so clear as when they are crystallized in a grade appeal. I know the panic I heard in Nancy's voice. I can imagine the nightmares she tells me she dreamt. If they weren't so radically unsettling, I would be glad for them. At least they make starkly clear what we are doing: we are grading one another.

10

Anorexia: The Cheating Disorder

I wanted to pray. A part of me would not let myself ask
Him for help. I did it to myself. God understood my confusion. I tried to figure out why it was happening to me, and
how. It only happens to weak girls, girls who have no self-
control, girls who are caught up with society's standards—
not me. But was I one of them? It was happening to me,
just like the cases I read about in magazines.

THIS IS THE first paragraph of an essay I received from a
young woman purporting to describe her own experience
with anorexia nervosa. Before I had finished reading one page, I
suspected it was plagiarized. I cannot easily explain my hunch.
Something canned about the writing, its confessional sentiment
exactly like the cases in the magazines. I ran a quick search
through the magazine index in the library, and then through recent issues of *Teen, McCall's, Glamour,* and *Mademoiselle.* In a
half hour, I had six articles: "Anorexia Nearly Killed Me,"
"Starving Oneself to Death," "Starving for Attention," "Two
Teens," "My Sister and I," and "One Teen's Diet Nightmare." I
did not accuse the student of plagiarism on the evidence of that
search, but I decided to talk with her before I would comment
on or evaluate her paper. I guessed that in our talk she would reveal that she had copied her essay or in some other way falsified
it. She did.

I am not inquiring here into the causes of plagiarism among
students nor describing how teachers ought to respond to it. I
am simply telling two stories in order to convey something of
the perverse experience of it.

Several years before I received the anorexia paper, a student submitted a brief analysis of James Joyce's "The Dead." As I was reading it, the paper tripped some wire in my mind. It seemed both accomplished and incompetent, full of discontinuities like those in the following two sentences:

> The physical movement of the main character, Gabriel Conroy, from a house in the western part of the city eastward to a hotel at the very center expresses in spatial terms his commitment to the ways and the doom of his fellow Dubliners. His spiritual movement westward, in our imaginative vision, symbolizes his supremeness of that doom through recognition of its meaning and acceptance of this truth of his inward nature.

Much of the first sentence here is sensible; the character's physical movement expresses his commitment. It is also syntactically sophisticated. The grammatical subject, "movement," is sustained through five prepositional phrases before its meaning is completed by the verb "expresses." The verb itself is modified by a prepositional phrase ("in spatial terms") that parallels and reiterates the adjective "physical." The second sentence, however, is nonsense. The grammatical kernel (movement symbolizes supremeness) is unintelligible. The pronoun sequence creates nothing but blur (his-our-his-that-its-this-his). One sentence, then, is substantial and coherent. The next is gummed with vagueness. So stark is the contrast between the two that it was difficult for me to imagine the same person writing both.

When I had assigned the paper, I explicitly restricted the use of secondary sources. I asked students to select a short reading from the literature we had been studying and to write an essay defining and explaining what they considered its central aesthetic purpose. I asked them to write about the work only as it presented itself to them in their reading. They were not to read or refer to any critical or historical background discussions of it.

In spite of the assignment's restriction, however, parts of this student paper about Gabriel Conroy seemed to me surely to have been copied. I scanned several library collections of critical essays on Joyce, browsed in longer works that made reference to *Dubliners*, and then, without having found anything but still

118

persuaded the paper was plagiarized, asked the student to come to my office to talk with me.

"Before I give you credit for this paper," I said, "I need to ask a couple of questions: Did you use any outside materials when you wrote this? Did you read any books or articles about Joyce or about this story?"

To both of those questions he answered no, simply and firmly. But the look on his face was perplexed, and I realized once again how difficult it is to confront plagiarism without proof, how important it is not to accuse a student of cheating without sufficient cause. I hurried to soften the impression that I thought he had cheated by saying that my reason for asking was the strange inconsistency in the paper between specific recounting of the story line and abstract discussion of thematic issues. I was trying to understand the combination, I said, and I thought that perhaps he had looked at some outside sources that had influenced what he wrote. He still looked puzzled, but said no again, and our brief conference ended.

Plagiarism irritates, like a thin wood splinter in the end of one's thumb. With any sort of reasonable perspective, I realize that one student's possibly copying part of one paper on James Joyce is a small matter. In a typical semester, I teach 120 students and read perhaps 600 student papers. In a typical day, I have two classes to prepare and teach, committee meetings to attend, conferences with individual students, the utility bill to pay, a child to pick up from a Cub Scout meeting. But everything I touch rubs the sliver in my thumb and sets its irritation pulsing. As much as I try, I cannot ignore it.

So when I happened to be sitting in a colleague's office, waiting for her to finish a phone call, my eye seized upon the book of Joyce criticism on her shelf. I had to look. It took only a moment. The phrases of the student's jumbled sentences were everywhere. I borrowed the book, took it back to my office, double-checked its lines with the lines of the paper, and then went again to the library.

I wanted to verify that our library collection contained the book and thus that it had actually been available to the writer. It was checked out. "To whom?" I asked. The circulation clerk said that library policy prohibited his divulging that information, but if I wished I could have the book recalled. I did, and reconciled myself to waiting several days for it to arrive.

In order to make the story complete, I have to explain some of the mixture of my feeling during this episode. Though I should not have had time to play detective, I made room among all the duties of my life to pursue this student. I was thrilled by the chase. When I happened on those sentences in my colleague's office, I was exhilarated. They promised the solution to a puzzle that had eluded me. They reinforced my sense of judgment and my sense of self-satisfaction at the thought that, in a small way, I was preserving the integrity of the university.

I was also dismayed, however, and angry, at what I came to feel as the obligation to play out the scene, at my exhilaration, at the student's distortion of our whole working relationship. When I thought about his voice, about his poise in denying that he had used any outside sources, I thought too about the other 119 students and wondered what his cheating meant about them. When I went into class in the following days and watched their faces, I realized that I had lost some of my faith in them. For no more reason than my experience with him, I found myself wondering what the rest of them had copied.

The recall notice came shortly afterward. I hurried to the library to pick up the book. When I could not find the sentences I was looking for, I first imagined that I had inadvertently recalled the wrong book. Then I thought that perhaps this was a different edition. I walked away from the circulation desk flipping the pages and wondering—through the electronic gate at the library door, out through the foyer past the philodendrons in their huge pots, onto the columned porch—and then I saw it. The gap in the pagination, page 98 followed immediately by page 113, and in the fold of the binding so neatly done as to be almost invisible, the seven razor-bladed stumps.

He still denied it, first in my office, then in the dean of students' office, sitting with his legs crossed in an upholstered armchair next to a whirring tape-recorder. He began by denying that he had even used the book, then that he had damaged it in any way, went so far as to say that he had noticed the missing pages and reported them to the library himself. He hadn't wanted to be blamed, he said. What kind of person did we think he was, he asked, how did we suppose he had been brought up? He was offended at the very thought of it. But when I finally left the hearing room, he admitted to the dean both that he had copied and that he had cut out the pages he had used. Within the week he was suspended from the university.

Every year I teach, I encounter students who cheat in their writing. Their stories are all different, and all the same: they were worried about their schoolwork, rushed, unclear about the assignment, afraid. My stories are all different, and all the same: an intuition, some feeling on the surface of the page, something about the dye of the ink that whispers this is counterfeit currency; then the excitement of judicial self-satisfaction, the slanderous suspicion that all my students are cheating. Though particularly vivid, my experience with the *Dubliners* paper is like all the others, obsessive and bilious. Like all the others, it has nothing whatever to do with what the job of teaching should be.

"Did this really happen?" I asked my student when we met to talk about her essay on anorexia. She was already nodding yes when I thought that I shouldn't seem rude in my disbelief. "I mean," I said, trying to make the edge of my question sharp, "I mean, did this happen the way you tell it here?"

"Yes," she nodded again. "Why do you ask?"

"Well, I don't know exactly." I looked up from the paper at her face, then back down to the typed page. "It's sort of vague in places, as if . . . I don't know . . . as if you didn't remember what happened in your own story."

Now she was shaking her head. "I don't know what you mean."

She played the correct gambit—my move, force me to commit myself. But I didn't want to move yet. I was after proof, and I needed to go after it slowly. This was a parody of a writing conference. I was asking her about the details of her story, trying to appear helpful, as if I were attempting to help her revise, when in fact I was trying to tease out the insincerity of her paper.

"I mean, I'm sort of confused by your essay," I said. "In the part here on page three where you say you ran to the bathroom to vomit—'I would run to the toilet to vomit, screaming the entire way' and 'The vomiting ceased after awhile'—when did that happen? Did that happen before you went to the hospital or after?"

"After."

"And here where you say, on page two, that your father stroked your hair and rubbed behind your ears, and then on the next page you say that your father was a monster who yelled at you and forced food down your throat constantly—are you talking about what caused your anorexia or what happened afterward?"

She didn't answer that question at all, just sat there looking at me, so I tried a different tack.

What struck me as I read and re-read her paper were the seams, the joints, where the parts were pushed together with no bonding. She is lying in a hospital bed staring at the ceiling tiles. She is trying to listen to the doctor talk to her. She is using and abusing a whole series of diet plans. She is flipping through a magazine looking at the pictures of models. She is taking a laxative every night before she goes to bed. She is listening to her father tell her that she is going home.

The effect on me was twofold. I thought that the details she included were completely credible—only a person who had lain in a hospital bed would think to mark off the ceiling tiles; only a girl whose father actually rubbed behind her ears would think to mention that specific caress. At the same time, the vague and abrupt transitions between these highly individual details seemed to me understandable only if I assumed that she had copied them in fragments from a magazine memoir. My guess was that she had taken them from an article that was too long to copy in its entirety and so had included just selected parts in her essay.

"Did you write this?" I finally asked unexpectedly. I did not plan to say it like that, but I couldn't seem to approach the real point of my questions by just skirting the issue.

Her face looked so blank that I immediately switched to a different question. "Is this story really about you?"

She paused for a moment, and then asked, quietly, "What would happen if it weren't?"

I told her that I could not accept such a paper since the assignment was to write about a personal experience of her own. I told her, too, that it would help explain the vagueness I had been trying to point out to her: if she wrote the paper about someone else's experience, then she would be likely to leave gaps in the story that she couldn't fill.

"What grade would I get on it if it were about someone else?" she asked. To pin me down.

"I wouldn't grade it at all. I wouldn't give you any credit for doing it. It's not the assignment."

"OK," she said. "It's not about me. It's about a friend of mine."

My reaction to her admission was complicated. I had been expecting it, in fact working toward it, trying to get her to tell me where the paper had come from. I was glad finally to have its pretense uncovered, but disappointed because I knew immediately that I would have to accept this substitute explanation though I didn't believe it either. I was sorry I had not been able to find the magazine story that provided the actual source of her paper and so would have to settle for this second lie about its roots. And I was angry at the whole situation: at the wasted time in the library, at the wasted conference with her, at my own inability to define the fakery of the piece, and at her apparent inability to see the purpose of our work together. I wanted her to write truthfully about her own experience and to use my responses, along with others', to help her convey the meaning of that experience more surely and vividly. As it was, her paper seemed just a hoax.

The deep flux of such feeling is just one of the dimensions for me of the problem of plagiarism. Another is the comic peculiarity of my claiming to be committed to helping students learn but sometimes spending large chunks of everyone's time trying to corner them in a fraud. Most troubling is the distance, the surprising separation I discover in such situations between myself and students. Because I assume their goodwill and candor and my own, both their cheating and my response to it shock me. I take for granted that we are working together and thus am amazed each time at the unimagined distance between us.

But even if I had expected the fakery of the anorexia paper,

I would not have been prepared for what happened. Even if I had remembered the pages sliced out of the book of Joyce criticism and the self-righteous posturing of that frightened student writer trying to elude me, I would not have anticipated the journal of the woman who had told me that her essay on anorexia was not really about herself, but about her friend.

I gave her a zero on the paper. She completed the rest of the semester's assignments, and at the end of the term, as required, she turned in a binder containing all her work for the course. As I was rereading her finished essays and the background notes and drafts she had made while working on them, I came upon the following entries in her journal:

> Feb. 7. My roommates and I did watch the Miss America pageant. I believe pageants are my favorite programs to watch. They are so inspiring. But sometimes that can make you sick.

> Feb. 21. The title of Miss America is such a distinguished title. Who ever is chosen for this honor represents the dreams of millions of young girls.

> Feb. 22. My next paper I am writing about when I had anorexia. The thought of going all through that again scares me but I think it would be a good experience to write about.

> Feb. 22. Skinny. Healthy. Slim. Muscle. Diets. Firmness. Roundness. All thoughts of women in today's society. Is this such a healthy attitude to have? Women can be obsessed with these listed thoughts to the point of worshipped, slimness, firmness, healthiness etc.—

> Feb. 22. . . . It really hurt.
> "You're fat" my brother said to me.
> I looked in the mirror.
> You're fat I said to myself.

> March 1. Blindness is a scary experience or at least it was for me. I haven't experienced blindness but something close to it. The world diminishes. Your only hope is through touch.

> March 2. Scared and alone, I laid in my hospital bed. I wanted to pray. I thought prayer would make me feel closer to the only friend I had left. My situation had done this to me. I thought it only happened to weak girls, girls who have no self-control, girls concerned w/society.

The journal entries astonished and appalled me. Their sincerity was unmistakable. These were not descriptions of a friend's experience. These were not fragments copied from the pages of a popular magazine. They were threads of memory—a brother's teasing, a father's touch. As closely as I can reconstruct it, she and I met in conference to discuss her essay on anorexia nervosa March 12, eighteen days after she began writing it, thirty-three days after she had begun to remember in her journal about the feelings that led both to her sickness and to her writing.

What must she have been thinking as I began to ask her those strange questions in our conference? At what point did she catch a glimmer of what I was really doing there? And when she saw it—if she saw it—what must she then have thought about it all—the course, me, the whole project of learning in school? What calculation, what weariness with it all, must have led her to deny her own paper? "Is this paper about you?" I asked her.

"No," she said.

I did not mean for it to come to this.

11

Symposium

EVERY FEW YEARS since 1968, I have received a letter or call from a boy I taught at Moreau High School. Then fifteen, he must be nearly forty by now. In sixth period he watched me pick up a pencil that had rolled off another student's desk and hand it back. "I'd never seen a teacher do that," he told me later, "be kind like that."

It was enough to make him want to reciprocate.

Many afternoons at school thereafter, the two of us sat together in my office or in the classroom or on the stairs at the end of the corridor. He taught me to play chess. In the evenings, he visited a chess club in Hayward, watched, played some, and then brought back the tricks he had seen. He overwhelmed me. He was so much stronger a player than I that we never got as far as the endgame, but it was bracing for me and so satisfying for him that he brought his small chess set to school every day.

I can see him still—black curly hair, short-sleeved shirt—leaning on his thin arm on the stair, looking down intently at the plastic board, waiting, waiting, then swooping up a piece and clapping it down on its new space with a smack.

His letters are handwritten in ballpoint ink on loose-leaf notebook paper, the pages crammed with words. Sometimes the envelopes themselves are covered with afterthought. His voice has the same insistence when he calls. He stands at a pay phone (I can hear the road traffic behind him) and races the operator to the three-minute mark, telling me as much as he can in the time he has about himself and the plight of man in the world.

I listen, thank him for calling, say it is good to hear his voice. But his calls and letters are difficult for me.

Part of the reason is that I no longer know him. He is married. He has children (two, I think). He works and lives in a city I have never seen.

Neither does he know me. I was a boy in 1968, a boy in a tie. We talked after school. He invited me to his parents' house; he visited mine. Then I left Moreau to enroll in a doctoral program, and he graduated. He has no more accurate a sense of me now than I have of him. And his words make me think he has less. Passionate disquisitions on the nature of society, long biblical quotations, prophetic statements about the duty of human beings in the modern world—his words orate, as if they were addressed homiletically to someone of like mind, or to no one. They seem completely impersonal. At the same time, they are so full of urgent respect for me that they embarrass.

I am his teacher still. He reaches his words out toward me as if I were still one of the most well-read, most thoughtful and inspiring people he has ever known. Sometimes he says as much. More often, for all their prolixity, his letters are reserved. Timid. His voice on the phone apologizes. Unable to speak to me as a person in the present, he wants a relationship that is past. It is a yearning I am unable to satisfy.

The relationship between teacher and student is sometimes so like love it disconcerts. Teaching writing and literature now at Radford University, I imagine I am simply fulfilling an institutional role. Sometimes I notice it is something more. I recoil, withdraw, straighten my tie. The same student stays after class day after day on one pretext or another. I listen, answer his questions, but I do not encourage him. I do not prolong our talk. Walking along Fairfax Street after an unusual Sunday afternoon meeting on campus, I see a young woman sitting beneath a tree near the sidewalk, apparently absorbed in a book. She is a student in one of my classes. Our eyes do not meet, but she appears again and again on the periphery of my days— along the regular path I take to my car, walking in the neighborhood of my house, in my rearview mirror. We do not speak; I do not let on that I notice.

When I was an undergraduate at the University of Santa

Clara, a student friend told me that she checked the class sched-ule of one of her teachers and scouted his daily itinerary. She wanted simply to see him, to cross his path. One day, he did the unimaginable. He stopped, spoke to her, congratulated her on winning an academic prize: "I hear they've created a medal for you," he said. And he smiled. Twenty-five years later, she can still see the other students walking by in the afternoon sun on Alviso Street, just between Kenna and Alumni House. She can see her teacher's black cassock and his white hair and his eyes squinting in the light. She can hear still his paradoxical voice—soft, yet clipped; gentle, but exact. In her mind, she runs her fin-gers still over his caressing words.

I admire the handsomeness of his gesture. I wish I could think to say such lasting, nourishing things. Yet that much influ-ence worries me. That much power. I want to be professional, ethical. I do not want to be courted or pursued through my days and years. Our eyes should not meet, I tell myself, and look away. We have nothing more to say (I think this while we are still talking), and I begin to devise ways to end the conversation, to disengage myself from their desire.

But.

I feel the desire myself. One spring afternoon, I walk out onto the front porch of the library and there, running in the dis-tance on Muse Lawn—I cannot quite believe it—is a naked girl. I shield my eyes from the sun and look more closely. No, she's not naked, after all. She has shorts on and a string bikini top, but I could have sworn . . . She was running to catch a Frisbee thrown from somewhere, but now she seems to me completely alone, the lawn deserted, she standing with her feet spread wide and her arms up, lifting her hair like a wild crown into the warm air. She is a silhouette, an apparition out of James Joyce, an angel of mortal youth and beauty. I feel her beckoning to me.

I say she was a girl. Some would say young woman. I am uncertain how to refer to her. She is a student in my class. She lies out on the grass in the midday sun, then comes to class poached, a loose T-shirt and shorts over her thin bathing suit. I concentrate on the work at hand, keep my eyes from lingering on the purple strings at her neck and hip. I appreciate her cover-ing herself, try not to imagine her otherwise.

Her modesty in class is a token. She and her friends, college students all over America these days, men and women, sunbathe nearly naked outside the windows of faculty offices. Here at Radford on the lawns of Moffett and Muse, for several weeks each year, the grass is covered with beach towels and books and bodies. Aristophanes might write an adaptation of *Lysistrata* to examine the ways in which the work of school is intertwined with the work of sex, a comedy of sexual harassment. I try not to notice, but I am less candid than the maintenance workers on the roof who stop spreading hot tar and stare.

I do not want to notice, but when I read a draft of a story I have written about Teresa Simpson to a small group of colleagues, one says, "You sound like you're in love with her."

"Oh . . ." I am unsettled. "Really? But that's not what I meant at all."

"Sure." He shrugs, smiles at my protest. "But look: the way you say her father stares at her, savors her hair and neck and shoulders, follows the line of light and shadow in her body in memory of her mother . . . see, that's *you* savoring her. And when she's in your office, settling herself in your chair, tucking her bare legs up . . . she is so physically present to you that it's obvious you're attracted to her."

"Oh, my goodness," I say, trying to sound as if I think we are talking about a writing problem, when in fact he is presenting me with a secret I have not even recognized in myself.

Its signs are everywhere. Teresa has the body I fashioned, red hair, sweater, voice and mannerisms. The same thing happens when I remember the evening Sandra Miyoshi sat late in my office reading to me about her grandmother in Hawaii. I pause at the scene. Brown shoulders, the inky blackness of her long hair—one strand stretching across the page of her paper—the whiteness of the page itself—the whole moment is charged in memory with sexual current. I rush to revise. I try to hide my own desire like an Aristophanic fool with an erection.

It would be just as well to admit it and accept it and inquire into its meaning: I want to love my students; I want to be loved by them.

This is not the same as being liked by them. I do not scorn

their liking, as some do, but it is not the same. If I construct courses with fresh variety, bring muffins to class (as my colleague, Nick Pappas, inspired me to do), smile a lot (freshman John McKinney said, "You're always smiling; I like that"), or bop around the room with contagious energy and cheer—if they like me for those things, I am glad. But I want more.

I want them to enter into my life. I want to enter into theirs. Reading Wilfred Owen's "Dulce et Decorum Est" in class, I am hoping for a moment when we will fall silent together, amazed beyond saying at the "old lie" about war. Reading *Hamlet*, I wait for a student to say quietly (though I fear for us both in wanting this) that she suspects it is her story, that she thinks her mother actually killed her father. I tell them I am Gabriel Conroy, shoes buffed and dinner speech notes in my pocket, self-conscious, middle-aged, wondering what it would have been like to have ever been young. When we puzzle together over "The Horse-Dealer's Daughter," I admit what I think at least is surely true: we kiss sometimes in order to avoid looking in each other's eyes.

A woman student who came back to college after years of work and a marriage that had dissolved, sitting in a room full of students the age of her grown children, told me she was amazed by the things I said in class.

"They are daring," she said. "Intimate." She was not being critical. She was thanking me. And then, unexpectedly, she reciprocated, in a story about her divorce, about the very moment it happened in her mind. One night after a banquet, back in an elegant hotel room (like Gretta and Gabriel in "The Dead"), she watched her husband's body emerge from his worn tuxedo, and she realized she felt no more loathing, nothing.

Intimate. The word comes from Latin (*intimus*, inmost, deepest). Often used with sexual connotation, its denotative meanings are more general and more profound. The intimate is the deeply private, the deeply personal viewed from the perspective of the self in relation to another person. The intimate is what is ordinarily not exposed, not shared with another, yet in its very definition it allows the possibility of exposing to, sharing with, knowing by another. The philosopher Michael Polanyi suggests that a large part of our knowledge itself is intimate. Not only is it what he calls "tacit," beyond expressing to ourselves or others. It is known by intimation (Polanyi helps us see that intimacy is active): we know by entering into what we know. We dwell in it. We participate in it imaginatively, feelingly. "Our knowledge of life," Polanyi says in *Knowing and Being*, "is a sharing of life—a reliving."

The subjects I teach—the reading of literature, the writing of expository essays—require of students precisely this kind of intimation. What does it mean, slipping on wet trunks after a summer rainstorm, to feel in one's groin the chill of death? What does it mean to remember in one's fingertips, with nameless grief, the labored breathing of a dying seal? One must enter into those moments of experience in order to understand them. I know no other way. One must love.

It seems to me just as true, just as necessary, that in order to understand the work of students in my courses, I must enter into *it* imaginatively, into *them*. When they read their papers to me, when they ask me questions or tell me stories—even when they lose heart or lie or cheat—it seems to me that teaching them is indistinguishable from loving them, whatever the frustration or satisfaction, suffering or joy.

There will be suffering.

A student comes into my office to read a draft of an essay in progress. He introduces it by saying he is very dissatisfied with the whole thing. I ask him to read, then we will talk. He does. I pause to think about my reaction. He cannot endure the wait.

"I think it's too wordy," he says. To fill the silence.

I think: what's the point of talking about its wordiness if he's dissatisfied with the whole thing? Why is he dissatisfied?

"Well, let me ask you this," I say. "What did you mean when you said you didn't like what you've got here? Is it what you're writing about that bothers you or how you're handling it or what?"

"Both. All. I just don't feel right about it."

I ask him what he wants to say, what he thinks *will* make him feel more satisfied.

Our exchange lasts maybe two minutes. Suddenly, he looks straight at me.

"Can we talk about my paper," he asks, "and not about me?"

I cannot answer immediately. I do not believe it will do him any good to talk about the wordiness of this draft. That is a side issue, less than a side issue, a diversion. I feel slapped by his question. I watch his face. Then I say, "Sure."

One semester I asked students to write in their journals about the course, to keep track of their thoughts and feelings about their work. They knew I would read what they wrote:

> Ya know, I used to really love English. Really love it. I still love reading, but you have made me hate it, and dread it. I'm not taking another English course Next year because I am afraid I might End up in another class like this. You have made me scared to learn, scared to take another course. You have shown me a darker side of English I never saw, Papers after Papers, Articles after Articles, Shit upon Shit. I'm never going to forgive you for this, Ever.

I was amazed by those words, battered by them, left soiled and trembling. I still see the student around campus who wrote them. We talk as if nothing had happened. He seems to have forgotten them. I have not. Some days his is the only face I see. I try not to look.

Every semester, students in my courses write evaluations of me and of my work with them—using either the official university system of anonymous written comments or writing me personal letters. After every semester is over, grades computed and recorded with the registrar, I brace myself and read what they wrote.

> I've been sitting here in my bare room for what seems like an eternity (oblivious of the time and the fact that I have two exams tomorrow) just staring at this blank piece of paper, trying desperately to pull my thoughts and feelings together in some logical order . . . . I think you're an excellent professor, Murph. You have a special talent for *teaching* and so much to give. You seem to

enjoy what you are doing and you do it well. . . . You have taught me so much—much more than British lit. and how to footnote a term paper correctly. You have taught me to look more closely at things (all things) and think seriously about what I see—from this I have learned more about myself. What can I possibly say? Bravo, Murph, and thank you.

I read the letter once, set it down, then read it over again.

We have all had teachers we loved—and love still in the memory of having worked with them. I have the notebook from Terry Loughran's ninth-grade history class. When we walked through the steam tunnel together on our way to the workshop to make models catapults, I walked just a step behind; he was my teacher, after all. I can remember his room, his books, his radio playing Vivaldi. I never wrote an evaluation for him, never told him. He does not know.

Seven years ago, I received the following letter. Though I quote only part, I think you will be able to sense something of its full effect.

Dr. Murphy:

Please understand that I respect you as a professor and admire your vast knowledge of literature. However, I feel that the course I completed this Spring in British literature was, at best, a disappointment.

My first complaint is about your attitude both during lectures and outside of class. As much as you professed to be open-minded in class and willing to listen to others' views and opinions, it became apparent that this wish was not genuine. I had listened to what classmates had to say about various poems, stories, etc., and felt that they often had valid suggestions to make to the group concerning the interpretation of the literature, only to find that if their ideas were not in line with what you were thinking, Dr. Murphy, you were quick to shrug it off or to dismiss it with a laugh which was not appropriate. As you are in a position of authority, I have no objections to your telling students what you believe is true; however, if we are to be responsible for and held accountable for *your* views and opinions, you should make this clear.

Also, I am not impressed with your idea of a test. I do not feel that literature that has not been discussed in class should be included on an exam covering the contents of a course. Also, I think that you should concentrate on the message that various works deliver, rather than on petty details which have little or no significance to the story.

I was not pleased to be scheduled for a conference at 9:20 p.m. You were obviously tired, as you yawned several times, and it really would have been better to postpone the appointment until a time when you were feeling more rested. Perhaps then you could have viewed my paper with a fresher outlook, rather than dealing with it as if it had fallen off an assembly line. I did not like your telling me that I did not mean to write a particular word in my essay, when indeed, I meant to use precisely that word. You were not the least bit encouraging to me as a writer. As a matter of fact, you were most discouraging. You have no right to tell others what they meant to say or what they did not mean to say. When evaluating an essay, you should not be concerned about whether you think the person has written what you think he feels or not, but should try to concentrate on what the person has actually written.

If this evaluation seems negative, that is because my reaction to the course was entirely negative.

Ms. E. Sanders

My grade book tells me that Ms. Sanders earned a B in that course. I cannot remember what she wrote her papers about (I marked them with B's, too). I have no face to go with her name (Ellen? Elizabeth?), no memory of the conference in which I yawned. But I have her letter.

I feel her fingers at my throat as I read, her nails in my eyes. I tell myself I do not deserve her contempt, but my self-justifications are pathetic. I keep them—and the anger and sadness—largely to myself.

So do my colleagues.

But sometimes our masks slip.

On the first day of class in September, a fellow teacher says to me, "Have you met the little bastards yet?"

One of my colleagues (students tell me) has a special-order stamp. He sets it out on his desk with mock glee whenever he begins reading a stack of student papers. The red stamp pad. The stamp with its shiny walnut handle. He looks like a mail clerk, pounding those papers as they pass beneath his eyes. A neat rectangle enclosing one word: "bullshit."

Listen to Jacob Neusner, a professor from Brown University. He wrote a graduation speech in 1981, submitted it to the student newspaper, then permitted it to be reprinted in newspapers and magazines across America:

> For four years we [the faculty at Brown] created an altogether forgiving world, in which whatever slight effort you gave was all that was demanded. When you did not keep appointments, we made new ones. When your work came in beyond the deadline, we pretended not to care.
>
> Worse still, when you were boring, we acted as if you were saying something important. When you were garrulous and talked to hear yourself talk, we listened as if it mattered. When you tossed on our desks writing upon which you had not labored, we read it and even responded, as though you had earned a response. When you were dull, we pretended you were smart. When you were predictable, unimaginative, and routine, we listened as if to new and wonderful things. When you demanded free lunch, we served it. And all this why?
>
> Despite your fantasies, it was not even that we wanted to be liked by you. It was that we did not want to be bothered, and the easy way out was pretense: smiles and easy B's. . . .
>
> That is why, on this commencement day, we have nothing in which to take much pride.
>
> Oh yes, there is one more thing. Try not to act toward your co-workers and bosses as you have acted toward us. I mean, when they do not give you what you want but have not earned, don't abuse them, insult them, act out with them your parlous relationships with your parents. This too we have tolerated. It was, as I said, not to be liked. Few professors actually care whether or not they are liked by peer-paralyzed adolescents, fools so shallow as to imagine professors care not about education but about popularity. It was, again, to be rid of you. . . .

My first reaction to this speech was astonishment. The current of Neusner's spleen ran so deep I was amazed that he would let it be known. He should stop teaching, I told myself piously, if that is what he thinks about students. But then, in the wide press coverage his words received, I heard the message that he was speaking for more than himself. He was speaking for us all. Teachers in Young Hall taped photocopies to their office doors for the edification of passersby.

I think of Ms. Sanders and the furious student who promised never to forgive me, and I realize that sometimes we are of like mind: we hate each other.

This should not surprise. It is love I am talking about. There are no guarantees. Our desire is deep, sometimes reckless, always insatiable.

In *The Symposium*, Plato's Aristophanes presents a comic myth to explain our desire. Human beings—originally whole, complete circles—were cut by the gods in two. Ever after, they have sought one another, desiring to reunite, to complete, to heal themselves. It is a ludicrous myth. Zeus is a bumbling god. Perfect humans are as odd as cartoons: one head, two faces, four hands and feet, two genitals. But this wild premise allows Aristophanes to describe the human condition with great precision: we cannot explain what we desire of one another. It is a yearning the soul cannot express. According to Aristophanes,

> the intense yearning which each of them has toward the other does not appear to be the desire of intercourse, but of something else which the soul desires and can not tell, and of which she has only a dark and doubtful presentiment.

Polanyi would call that presentiment an intimation. Just as he would say it cannot be expressed, Plato would say (through Aristophanes) that it cannot be fulfilled. We are human. We are divided, incomplete. It is the comic rendition of our fallen state. We are not what we desire to be in memory or dreams. "Human nature was originally one," Aristophanes says, "and we were whole, and the desire and pursuit of the whole is called love."

The comedy of school is that it is so ill-designed for love. Our reaching into and out of ourselves is scheduled by a computer. We meet one another two or three days a week for a semester. Reading this poem or writing this essay is one requirement in a list of others which teacher and student both check off upon completion.

"OK, people. This is essay number seven. Just two more and we're done."

"I still need nine hours to graduate, so I'll be going to summer school."

"Eleven semesters. That's it. Eleven more semesters, and I can retire."

From the point of view of love, the very structure of school is ironic. Teacher and student are strangers. Their paths cross for a moment, by chance. Even as they approach one another, they are drawing apart. And if that were not the system already, we would want it to be so. For all our desire, teachers and students do not want to love each other. Can we talk about my paper, please, and not about me? We look closely at each other, and then we look away.

Sometimes, however, our small bit of work together is so fine that it transfigures the business of school and seems to satisfy the inarticulate yearning of our souls.

A student wrote to me once to tell me what she had learned. In her letter, she did not mention me or the work at all. Instead, she told about a walk she had taken alone one winter dusk into the mountains behind her home. Everything was quiet, deserted, frozen in beauty. Beyond a shed, past a ridge, into the valley of a stream running black, she traveled. Dimly, she recognized the danger in it, in the cold and dark. She knew she was beyond any call for help. Finally, she stopped. Stood still. Listened to the water. Let the night fold her up. When she got back home, neither her mother nor her sister asked where she had been or what she had done. It was good that they didn't, she wrote, because she would have been unable to explain. It was just that up there in the woods alone that night, she felt connected to absolutely everything. And she hoped I would understand. I do.

Yet it is still difficult for me to know how to reply to her or to the boy who was my student many years ago at Moreau High School. We knew one another for a short while, talked and worked together, loved one another. Then we grew apart. Neither of us has forgotten. We played chess together after school in the stairwell. He said that I was the kindest teacher he had ever known.

12

Teachers

I WAS TWENTY-SEVEN years old when George Wallach first encouraged me to tune up my own car. He had a Volkswagen himself, said the job was simple and economical, and volunteered to come over to our house on Fifty-fifth Avenue one Saturday morning to walk me through the process. He recommended I buy a book—*How to Keep Your Volkswagen Alive: A Manual of Step by Step Procedures for the Compleat Idiot* by John Muir—and he rode with me down to Sears to buy the tools I needed and to Grand Auto for the parts—distributor points, spark plugs, and several quarts of oil.

Walking me through the process meant walking *next* to me through the process, not leading me, certainly not doing it *for* me. First thing, I was on my back on the concrete floor of the garage under the left rear wheel well of a '66 Bug. George said, "Find the wire spring holding the valve cover."

"What does it look like?" I asked.

"Like a bent coat hanger." George was standing in the sun in our driveway, hands in his pockets. I was trying to get my eyes to focus in the dark on the underside of the car. Everything looked the same, caked with road crud, mysterious. I took an inventory of these strange things—the inside of the rear wheel, the flat thing with ridges in the middle of the rear end, the shiny tail pipe leading in from the bumper and disappearing at a clamp into something else. I finally ran my fingertips gingerly over the surfaces, and then suddenly there it was, right behind the tire, the coat hanger/valve cover spring I was looking for.

"Pry it up with the screwdriver," George said.

I slipped the screwdriver shaft under the spring and lifted. Nothing. I pressed against the handle. It slipped. I reset the screwdriver blade against the surface of the cover and pressed up again. Nothing.

"How hard do I have to push to get this thing off here?"

"Harder."

The caked mud was breaking free and crumbling into my face. I could not seem to find an angle for my body so that I could put enough shoulder behind the screwdriver's leverage.

I said, "I need to turn around, George. I can't get at it this way."

"OK," he said. I had the fleeting impression that he knew, twenty minutes before, that I would not be able to get anything done lying under the car with my feet alongside the tire. But I was preoccupied with the valve cover, so I did not stop long enough to be embarrassed. I slid back under the car on my left shoulder, my legs stretched out to the rear, grabbed hold of the screwdriver handle with my right fist and pried and grunted and pushed.

The sprong of its breaking open, amplified by the wheel well, exploded in my ears as if I were inside a church bell. All that resistance suddenly giving way made my right arm numb. I lay there with it extended, holding the screwdriver, until I was able to realign myself and slip the blade out from under the lifted spring. My right hand was in shock. I had been pressing against the screwdriver with hand-arm-shoulder-hip, torquing my body into the work, so that when the spring gave way, there was no way to call my hand back. It flew up into the wheel well, smashing against the mud-coated metal. My bleeding fingers still clutched the screwdriver on my chest as I waited for the trembling to calm.

"I got it," I said.

"Good," said George.

I decided to tell him.

"I hit my hand pretty hard, trying to get that loose . . ."

"Yes," he said. "You have to be careful there."

That's the way it went. Pulling off the valve cover and spilling oil on the sleeves of my shirt. Tightening up the lock nut on the number one intake valve and discovering with the feeler gauge that *again* it was too loose. Tuning up my car was full of peril. The nine-millimeter nuts on the oil screen cover could be stripped in a second. Every time I got the point gap right, I ran the risk of moving the plate when I tried to screw it down and of having to loosen it and reset the points once more.

George was taciturn through it all.

"Do I have this right?" I would ask.

"Does it feel right?" he would say.

I think I wanted something like sympathy. I know I wanted more than he gave me. I wanted him to tell me when I had done a job well enough, but he refused. Always the question came back to me. I had the feeler gauge; I had the timing light; I had to measure and decide. I wanted him to permit me to yell "SHIT!!!" when I burned my fingers on the hot drain plug and dropped it into the pan full of dirty oil. But there was something about the way he stood there in the driveway with his hands in the pockets of his coat, that made me think yelling would not do much good anyway. I had the sense that he already knew about mashed, burned fingers and jobs stalled out for lack of a nine-millimeter nut.

"Yes," George would say. "Gotta be more careful there."

At first, his sanguine look annoyed me, but that didn't appear to trouble him either. You want to tune up your car? It's a simple job. You have to cultivate patience.

For twenty years, Richard Rodriguez has been laughing at me, teasing, mocking my misguided ways. From the start, when we were both new graduate students at Berkeley, Richard said I was too serious. I did not sufficiently realize the goodness of Susie and my children. My agnostic Catholicism was just the product of having spent too long imagining gray old England. What I needed was the Mediterranean.

"We all fart, you know," he said on the way into a seminar on Spenser. "That's what this allegory we're reading is about, child."

Child. It was one of his diminutives. It irked me. It implied that I did not know my family, my religion, my body; they all belonged to him.

We both attended a noontime course in medieval English

140

literature, sharing my paper bag lunches—salami sandwich, potato chips, an apple—then walked out talking. One day we had a guest lecturer, reading and talking to us about anonymous lyric poems.

"Awful," Richard hooted afterwards. "Ridiculous. Call that teaching . . . ?"

I interrupted him. Though I, too, thought the class meeting had been inert, bloodless, I defended the guest lecturer. I pointed out that he was learned, that he read well.

"It's not *his* job to jazz up the poems," I said. "Presumably, we are there to develop our own appreciation . . ."

"When *that's* what appreciation looks like . . . ?" Richard interrupted me in turn, exasperated.

Our talk always accelerated: civil turn-taking, interruptions, talking over each other's voices, sometimes (when we were luckiest) building joint sentences in a rush of shared insight.

Then he finished, implicating me too (as usual) in his amused indictment: "When *that's* appreciation, the best they can hope for is . . . you. Andy Hardy, boy critic."

He got under my skin. Passing the student union, he said he had to stop in for a minute to look at *Women's Wear Daily*, wanted to see what Pat Buckley was up to. Not *Publications of the Modern Language Association*. Not *The Yale Review*. *Women's Wear Daily*.

"What sort of pose is this?" I asked. He countered with that rumbling laugh of his: "You think life is distilled in the Wheeler Hall English department?"

He told me I owed myself more expensive shirts: "It'd broaden your mind to wear one, just once."

One afternoon at a cafe on Telegraph Avenue, I tried to talk with him about the paper I was writing on "Dover Beach." He said, more patient this time than teasing, "You're *good*" ("good" was another diminutive) "but I hope you're going to say somewhere why the poem matters." Many of our teachers did not care about that, he said, but *we* should. Then he told me a story. In a seminar meeting at Columbia with Saul Bellow, all the graduate students around the table had done their little thing when Bellow asked the question that still echoed for Richard: "Doesn't anybody in this room *care* that Hector *died*?"

See Fellini, Richard told me, and Lena Wertmuller. "*Seven Beauties*. It'll remind you of Catholicism." Read Oriana Fallaci's *Interview with History*. Go to Rome.

"For God's sake," I finished with what I thought his impatient voice would say.

He corrected me again: "For your sake."

He was easy, eloquent. He had time to reread *The Faerie Queene* over the weekend ("Reread?" I asked in amazement, still plodding my way for the first time through Book III; it seemed a physical impossibility: no eye and mind could get through the poem that fast). He spent the morning writing a twenty-page paper (what could "writing" mean, I wanted to know, if that were so). He spent the afternoon drinking coffee and talking at a cafe table, stopping by the butcher's on his way home to buy lamb for his dinner and flowers for his apartment. He pretended that Berkeley was Europe (one evening, driving at dusk with me down Claremont Avenue toward Ashby, he exclaimed that he had seen just that rose light over Paris), and it was.

His public manner was reserved. When he spoke in class, his hands trembled. His voice was soft and halting. He finished speaking one afternoon with an apologetic laugh, "Does this make any sense?"

"Does it make any sense?" Paul Alpers, the seminar leader, repeated with undisguised admiration. "Sure. I wish I had said it myself."

I went to Rome and Florence at Richard's behest, to New York, to Paris. I read the writers he recommended: Hugh Kenner, Samuel Beckett, Augustine, Tillie Olson. ("Don't you read *anything*?" he asked, then answered his own question in mock disgust. "No, of course not.") Our talk stretched across the afternoons and the years. He admits he baited me; he calls my replies Jesuitical. We argued about everything: torture, wealth, time, friendship, teaching.

As angry as he sometimes made me, I was enchanted. He was interviewed for a Fulbright fellowship by a selection committee at Berkeley. Afterwards, laughing, he told me that he talked about a picture he had seen in the Uffizi, Caracci's *Bac-

chante. That was the topic he had gotten them to discuss, the lushly seductive back of a nude woman, glorious in its sensuality, full to the light. By his own account, Richard had cast a spell over the moment, dissolved the university agenda, turned the conversation where he wanted. I tried to resist his picture of that committee, charmed by easy frankness, but I could not. I was charmed, too.

I wrote a dissertation on the theory of poetic justice as it was developed in France and England at the end of the seventeenth century. I spent months in the rare book room of the Bancroft Library reading Andre Dacier, Rene Le Bossu, Rene Rapin, Thomas Rymer, John Dennis—in French and in English. I wrote my dissertation in the graduate students' carrel room on the third floor of Wheeler Hall on yellow scratch paper in tiny, black letters. Three years: two drafts. Richard went first to the Warburg Institute in London, then—bypassing Wheeler Hall and the Berkeley English department and dissertations altogether—back to a one-room apartment in San Francisco. There he wrote *Hunger of Memory,* the story of his education, of his learning to read, of his choosing what mattered to him. Many years: innumerable drafts, his hand scrawling across the page. Its first words inscribe the lesson he had been trying to teach me all along:

"I have taken Caliban's advice. I have stolen their books. I will have some run of this isle."

Ralph Rader directed my dissertation on poetic justice. I asked him to help me because I appreciated both the clarity of his talk and the vigor of his mind, and what seemed to me to be his integrity as a person. In an English department in which some of his colleagues aspired to academic glamour or rarefied fame, I found Ralph's lack of affectation wonderfully refreshing. He prized common sense and sharp candor, and he cultivated in himself a deeply passionate imagination. When he read Browning's dramatic monologue "Porphyria's Lover" aloud in class, we could recognize its madness in his chilling voice. Once, during a faculty discussion of lyric poems he suddenly began reciting lines from the medieval poem "The Wanderer," his face transfigured with their longing. He explained that his research into the genesis of two of Tennyson's love poems grew out of his

143

conviction that they derived from a previously unknown love affair that Tennyson must have had in his youth. (He was *sure* of it, he told us; just reading the poems made him certain.) Yet another day in class, he reproduced the exhilarating confirmation of Einstein's hypothesis that light should be affected by gravity. (He was trying to illustrate for us the power of explanatory hypotheses in literary interpretation.) With his face and body—both undistinguished, short and round, but deployed with the nuance and flourish of a resourceful actor—he recreated Eddington's 1919 expedition to photograph the solar eclipse. There in front of a literature classroom he drew with his hands the parhelion of Mars at the rim of the darkened sun. In his face we could read the wonder of the research team as their developed photographs provided the measurements by which Einstein's prediction was so elegantly confirmed.

Like Boswell in the presence of Samuel Johnson (Ralph called it "the Boswell effect"), he projected his imagination into whatever he saw and heard, contemplated it with rapture, strove to understand it from within. He was intense. His sentences struggled for clarity, the spoken ones half uttered then revised in mid-delivery, the written ones unrolling in polysyllabic subordination, qualifications striving toward precision. Sometimes his face was suffused with worry. His eyes would narrow, his lips purse, all his features pulled together in a momentary grimace of physical anxiety. Even more than anxiety, the look seemed to me to express disapproval as well, of something, of himself.

A teacher at Berkeley offered a course one time in Samuel Beckett. Somewhere—perhaps in his posted course description—the teacher said that he did not know much about Beckett but hoped to take this opportunity to learn more. Ralph and I were at the door of his office when I saw his face pull into that grimace of disdain. "Doesn't know much about Beckett?" he said. "Then what business does he have teaching the course?"

I saw the same expression one day I dropped by his office at the very beginning of a term. He was sitting at the end of the short seminar table squeezed into the middle of the room, a worn copy of *Tom Jones* open in front of him. He was worrying about his first class. "I *never* feel good about it," he said, and then punctuated the "never" with that sharp look of dismay.

But it was the first day of class that made me want to be his student. Fall 1970, English 208, Problems in Literary Methods. Ralph outlined the course work: we were each to choose a single, short, great, modern lyric poem—"Dover Beach," "The Windhover," "Leda and the Swan," a handful of others—and spend the term studying it. Then he turned to the crux of the course: literary form. Suddenly I realized the man was *arguing*. First day, general course structure out of the way, he was *advocating* something. I was not sure what it was. I did not know who he was contending with. But when he spoke, it was with a voice I heard again and again in the seven years I was his student: deeply, unaffectedly, impatiently passionate.

He talked quickly that first day, as he often did, his sentences spilling out over each other, unfinished, emphatic. When one of us said something, Ralph looked intently at the speaker, his eyes open and tranquil, his mouth relaxed, his body still. Then he darted at what was said, with his high, dry voice, in a sharp fragment of a sentence: "yes, YES. I think SO." Or, "and see where THAT's gotten us."

He picked up the pointer from the chalk ledge, waved it, laid it over his shoulder like a broom handle, dangled it out in front of him between two fingers and let it swing as he talked. He did not think he had pinned down the truth, but he thought we could get a lot closer to it in literary studies than we had so far. Studying literature was like reading the mind, and as complex a task as that is, Ralph said, he wanted to try to establish some of the points about which "we *must* agree." He had an intimation (it was from Ralph that I first heard of Polanyi and of personal knowledge)—a hunch about poems and our reading them together, teacher and students. His desire to bring that intimation to light was vast. His thick fist closed around the pointer and slammed down on the desk next to him: an exclamation point enacted.

As cerebral as his teaching was, it was intensely physical. The antacid tablets he sometimes chewed left traces of chalk on his lips. At the beginning of one lecture, he discovered a pack of cigarettes on the lecturer's table. "Somebody take these, will you?" he asked with a laugh that was half self-reproach. "Otherwise, I'll smoke them all before I even notice what I'm doing." On my way to a party at the end of one course, I met him on the sidewalk as he was getting out of his car.

"Don't you want to lock it?" I asked.

"No," he said simply, making his dismissal of vandals or car thieves a point of pride. "I don't want to do them the courtesy."

One spring I joined with other students to nominate Ralph for a distinguished teaching prize. I had enrolled in and audited several of his courses. For years he had been reading my writing and talking with me about it, and I had been watching him as a teacher and as a person. Again and again I had been the recipient of his kindnesses. He told me not to worry about being too sick to finish a paper. Get yourself well first, he said; that's more important. When I was lost and ready to quit the program, he counseled me back to confidence and hope. He asked only one question during my oral qualifying exam, a crucial question, to get me out of a snarl of explanation I was making for myself. He knew I knew the answer; in his question I recognized him reaching out his hand. In my last spring at Berkeley, he had become department chairman. Knowing how interested I was in teaching and how much I enjoyed it, he recommended that the Bay Area Writing Project invite me to be one of its summer fellows. In doing so, he gave my career as a college teacher its initial direction and coherence.

But, as grateful as I was for his personal kindness, I nominated him for the teaching award for other reasons. For one thing, his classroom was eclectic. Eighteenth-century novels, modern physics, "The Mary Tyler Moore Show," Kuhn and Popper on science, the first film version of *The Godfather*—Ralph would roll and unroll the short sleeves of his shirt and get us talking together about them all.

I was moved too by the way his spirit would suddenly flash out in the midst of whatever we were doing. When I was working with him on a study of "Dover Beach," he shared with me some of his own notes about the poem. Out of his neo-Aristotelian terminology and involved syntax emerged a sudden surprise. He wrote: "The fact that we would desire a better 'fate' for the speaker if we did not perceive that as impossible generates the thrilling poignancy which is the effect: the investment in desire, rendered unnecessary, is discharged and felt as 'painful pleasure.'" The surprise for me was that thrilling poignancy. It was what I felt as I watched him struggle to know.

He also seemed courageous to me. I once heard him read a paper on lyric form to a group of English department faculty and students. In the question period following his reading, one member of the audience asked if it were not possible to read Tennyson's "Ulysses" as an ironic dramatic monologue.

"No."

No hemming and hawing, no waffling.

Straight answer: "No. If it were possible, then the claim I am making about its lyric form would be refuted."

A reckless reply. It invited everyone in the room to dismiss what he had labored to present. It opened him to the charge that his argument was simply special pleading, that he was refusing to consider possibilities that would interfere with the conclusions he wished to draw. He accepted that criticism, understood its inevitability, and stood his ground. I loved him for it.

I thought I heard some of my own words repeated in the citation read at the teaching award ceremony. He was a stubborn teacher, with neither arrogance nor presumption. He was a performer, without affectation. He was straightforward with students, and toughly critical, without ever being mean or condescending. It was the opinion of all the people I knew who knew him: he was uniquely eloquent, generous, and unassuming, a teacher of special power and merit.

Every day that I think about teaching, I am reminded of one of these three of my teachers. Or of others. Terry Loughran, Wayne Shumaker, Bruce Klickstein. Sister Jean Bernard, who taught me for three years at St. Lawrence O'Toole's and who, in making me write reports on Marconi and draw maps of the Mediterranean, first helped me to like school. Brother John Perron, a fellow teacher at Moreau High School, who helped me realize that I could talk with students about Erich Fromm and Paul Tillich and who helped me learn on the job what sort of teacher I wanted to be. Then, too, a man whose name I can't remember, our high school sociology teacher: the summer before I started college, he invited four of us to his Oakland apartment one night a week to study Latin with him. And there are more who themselves have disappeared from memory but whose lessons endure, orphaned, at the center of my life and work.

If I could gather them all together, they would look like the teachers squeezed around the tables in Tolman Hall for the Bay Area Writing Project. Jim Gray, the project director, had invited thirty teachers from all grade levels, kindergarten through college. He asked us to share with one another our ideas about teaching writing. It was the best classroom I'd ever been in. We paired up to do dictation the way students in Linda Schwimmer's ninth grade did. Rebekah Kaplan taught us about Francis Christensen's cumulative sentences and got us writing some, appositives accumulating all over the room. We drew with finger paints on large pieces of butcher paper taped to the floor the way the children in Linda Kroll's elementary class did. In the process, we talked about our pictures and told one another the stories they represented. Fran Claggett brought up Robert Duncan's early book of poems, *Derivations*, and recommended that we assign students derivative writing, deliberately imitating the subject and style of a writer we admired. Her presentation inspired Jim Gray to propose an impromptu contest: pick a paragraph from a writer you like and insert a sentence of your own; the paragraph with the most seamless insertion wins. (The prize was a copy of Mina Shaughnessy's new book *Errors and Expectations*.) Working with the teachers of the Bay Area Writing Project delighted and inspired me. At the same time that they introduced me to many books and ideas and instructed me to think in new ways about writing and classrooms, they made me feel privileged to be their colleague.

It's how I think of my own teachers. It's how I think of Susie. We began teaching at the same time, she in second grade, I in high school. While I went through graduate school, she continued to teach. I watched in admiration and envy as her classroom flowered with invention and intelligence. First, it was book boxes—grocery-store produce cartons that she elaborately decorated to look like dog houses and lions' heads and packed with children's books on different themes. Then it was Lyle the Crocodile. Susie and a fellow teacher so enjoyed the Lyle books written by Bernard Waber that they developed a whole classroom fantasy using the character of Lyle. They pretended that every evening when they and the children were gone home, Lyle would visit the classroom and leave huge, floor-to-ceiling letters to be read the next day. Every day for a week or more, Lyle would visit and write; sometimes he would even answer the children's questions if they left him a note. Then it was chocolate chips. To introduce estimation and to provide practice in counting, Susie filled a large clear jar with foil-wrapped Hershey's kisses and asked the children to guess the number of candies. She graphed the frequency of the different estimates, then emptied the kisses, counted them, and passed them around to be eaten. Variations on that theme—how many raisins are there in these Sun-Maid boxes? how many chocolate chips are there in these cookies?—led her to begin cooking in class, too. Have the children make a batch of chocolate chip cookies, bake them in the cafeteria oven, then eat them carefully and count. Hers was a classroom in which learning was happening everywhere.

She was indomitably resourceful. Assigned to makeshift portable classrooms at one time, she and a fellow teacher talked the principal into allowing them to cut a hole in the wall between the two buildings so that they could team teach their two classes. Another time, when she was teaching kindergarten, she somehow arranged to have a wooden play structure built inside her room. Suddenly then, in the midst of everything else, the children in her class had a loft for reading and a stage for puppet shows and a corner for working in small groups on individual projects.

During all the years Susie taught elementary school, our house became the workshop for her classroom. Poster board, construction paper, brightly colored yarn, aluminum foil, different colored markers, yards of contact paper, and bottles and bottles of glue—many nights these materials covered our living room floor and dining room table. Though often she reused the things she made (she made them so durably they would last), more often she was making new things, so her classroom grew more and more dense with color and splash. Mammoth calendars for the bulletin boards (that she refused to buy ready-made from the teacher supply companies), mobiles hanging from the light fixtures, signs large and small for everything from light switches to scissors boxes, graphs, poems, giant chocolate chips —the room burst with life. She made a rug for one corner from patches of carpet remnant, taping its pieces together at home; its irregularity added to the cheerful motley effect of the room. She printed out recipe cards for the children's next day's cooking—enriching the mathematics of counting and measuring with nutritional awareness and a beginning recognition of cultural difference. For the Mexican festival Cinco de Mayo, they cooked tortillas and beans, for Chinese New Year, stir-fried vegetables. Some days she brought so many things from home to school, she needed help getting all of them into and out of the car and up to her classroom.

Today, when Susie advises student teachers about working with children in school, she says, "*Play* with them." It's a simple rule, and it conveys something of the exhilaration with which she taught. But it is also misleading. She may seem to be recommending simply fun. What she is recommending is work. I watched her. Late nights, planning and preparing, endless hours cutting out shapes and printing instructions. Her teaching was deeply mindful. The cooking connected to the bulletin board and the geography lesson, to the song the children learned to sing and the story she read to them on the rug after lunch, to the costume she wore and the guest she invited to visit. The whole was wonderfully orchestrated, highly organized, encyclopedic, and fascinating.

She gave me the same advice the morning I went off to teach my first Freshman English class at Berkeley. As a graduate student assistant, I had been asked to conduct the two weeks of class discussions of *I Henry IV*. I knew very little about Shakespeare; I knew even less about the play. I had never read it. I was familiar with Falstaff from hearsay, but had no sense at all of the play's plot or its historical and political background. After reading the play and some of the criticism and scholarship written about it, I decided to focus the first day's discussion on establishing the principal characters and the general facts of their story.

I had no idea whether such a plan was a good one, but I guessed that it would be helpful to subsequent discussions of the play if the students and I all started from the same facts. I winced as I heard in my mind the echo of Ralph Rader's "What business does he have teaching it anyway?" about the teacher who did not know very much about his subject. This was college, and Berkeley at that. What could I presume to say about *Henry IV?* Richard Rodriguez laughed at our teachers, and at me for wanting to defend them and then become them. "Students deserve to have us *care* about these things," he said in exasperation. But it was not exactly care I felt about the text I was assigned to teach; I was just trying to figure it out. However uncertain I was about my lesson plan, I knew that looking at the play was a good thing. Who is this Hotspur? What is it that he wants? Like lying on my back and looking up at the underside of a Volkswagen engine, it seemed to me that just staring at the play together for a while would help things come clearer. "Is this right?" I asked George. "Does it feel right?" he asked back. Well, no, as a matter of fact. This is my first class, and I'm pretty nervous about it. I had done all the work I knew how to do, made all the notes, planned all the questions, charted the hour, looked the text over once more, and still I was nervous.

As we parted that morning, each of us to our different schools to teach, Susie smiled and said, "Play with them."

And that's what I did.

13

Sursum Corda

For Christmas 1943, two years before I was born, my mother gave my father a gold signet ring. She died in 1958. When my father remarried, he packed up many of her things, including the ring, and stored them in the back of his bedroom closet in Oakland where they remained for the rest of the time my brothers and sisters and I were growing up.

Slowly over the years, with patience and love, my stepmother, Norma, helped my father go through those memories, to decide what he wanted to keep, give away, or discard. When he came upon the ring, she urged him to give it to me. Forty years later.

Memory surprises. As soon as I slipped the ring on my finger, I saw his hands.

To the eyes of a boy, they were thick hands, thick-fingered, soft and clean. When we were getting ready for church, he was always dressed first, standing in the living room by the fireplace, cleaning the arcs of his nails with the edge of a matchbook cover.

His hands made me want to smoke and drive. They caressed a cigarette and a steering wheel. L&Ms were his brand when I first remember him smoking, the thin white line of the cigarette between his fingers or cupped next to his palm. When I woke up at night as a child in the back seat of our family's humming Plymouth sedan on the way home to Oakland from San

Francisco, the only things I could see among the shadows were the profile of his face in the amber lights of the Bay Bridge and his soft hands up near the top of the wheel.

I do not remember his ever spanking me when I was growing up. I do not know if my memory of that is accurate, but I know now something I did not know then: that he was raised in a family steeped in hatred and violence, and vowed that he would never make a house like that for his own children.

When he wrote, he had the habit of stretching out the fingers of his left hand on the page, as if to smooth it out, as if to hold it down. Sometimes he would make the same gesture in speech. Looking intently, his head cocked a little to the side, he would reach a hand into the air, stretch his thick fingers wide and thereby clear the space between them and press his words toward his listener.

At all those moments, I saw the ring with his initials. When he gave it to me—because the initials are mine, too—smoothed down, worn, it brought back my childhood. When I put it on my hand, I saw his.

And then I lost it.

I am not certain where, but I think it was in a camp site in northern Michigan along the shore of Lake Superior. Susie, the children, and I were trying frantically to decamp during a summer rainstorm. Many hours and miles later, when we had finally stopped in a gray Laundromat to dry our sodden equipment and to try to raise our spirits, I discovered the ring was gone. I imagined it flying off my finger as I hurriedly pulled down a tent or shook out a ground cloth. For a moment, I pictured myself going back over the muddy area square foot by square foot, feeling every inch of the place, while my family waited in the car, the closed windows fogging up in the rain. But I thought that for just a moment. I cannot reconstruct all the sources of my desolation at the time, but there was no going back. The ring was gone, and we were going forward, driving into the waste and rain of central Canada.

If I had it to do over again, I would go back. I have thought many times since that I should have. It meant too much to me to let it go that easily. Where did that instant resignation come from? Why didn't I ask my family to let me drive us back? Why didn't I just turn around and do it?

One evening, after a faculty dinner here at Radford University, a colleague asked me how I sustained my enthusiasm for teaching. The question startled me. Why would he imagine that I could? What must he have thought he saw in me? What must he have been implying about his own experience as a teacher if he looked to me for enduring enthusiasm?

I told him that some days the job of teaching seems nothing more than fraud. A massive institutional con game. I feel unprepared, the students indifferent. Some days my dejection is so sharp it paralyzes me. I sit stupidly before the computer screen and hold my sides and try to breathe very slowly. I think I should quit, we all should quit, stop pretending to do this thing we call school and try to find something we believe in.

I am not alone in this feeling.

A small group of us recently got together to discuss what we loosely called the "academic environment" of our campus. Like all faculties everywhere always, we were concerned that students seemed distracted from their studies by life in the dorms, by emphasis on the social calendar, by programs of comedians and rock concerts that appeared frivolous to us. There were other issues, too, more specifically academic: library hours that seemed too limited, midsemester vacations that started early and ended late for many students, class sizes too large to permit us to assign students much writing or to give what writing we assigned close attention, a policy for dropping courses that encouraged students to carry more courses than they were actually working in, only to drop them at the last minute. We did not make this list up ourselves. It had been talked about for some time in halls and workrooms, over lunch or beer.

Our meeting to discuss the academic environment was unofficial. Faculty were invited by word of mouth. I do not know how far the word spread, but only four of us came, of a faculty of about four hundred. We complained for a while to each other, argued listlessly about whether grades were really necessary, and then left. It was a sad, pathetic meeting. The four of us, around a large wooden conference table, trying to define our sense of failure.

"I don't know what to do with them," one teacher said. "Don't know how to motivate them. Don't think I should have to."

Nods, murmurs of agreement: this is college, after all, isn't it?

He went on: "One guy comes in, sits in the back of the room, opens up the newspaper and reads. All through the class. Sits there with the paper opened wide and reads. I'm lecturing; he's reading. That must be a distraction to the other students. I know it's a distraction to me. I'm trying to lecture and this guy doesn't give a damn about what I'm saying."

Somebody in the group said, "Why don't you talk with him about it?"

"Can't. You can't tell a guy to stop reading the paper . . ."

I was amazed by the helplessness of his voice, by the weariness of his answer. Sure you can, I wanted to say. You just do it. You just walk up to him and say, "Listen, here's the deal: this is a class in session; you're distracting me and probably other students; you want to read the paper, read it somewhere else, some other time." You don't have to do it rudely. You can make it a request, you can present it courteously, but you don't have to go on day after day watching him ignore the class.

But I did not say any of that. I watched his face sag and his sweatered body slump in his chair. He has taught twice as long as I. He is a senior member of the faculty here. What I think he saw reflected in the back of that student's opened newspaper was his own failure. What I think he sensed was that his lecture was worthless. He could not force a showdown because the student would silence him with a single sentence: "As soon as you say something I think's worth remembering, I'll write it down."

I too have been seared by such moments. What looks like a simple exchange with a student suddenly becomes an indictment of my whole life as a teacher. It is not just my body but my mind that flags at such moments, and the trembling in my muscles sickens me with shame.

After my father died, my stepmother gave me the cardboard box in the back of his closet. It contained the last traces of his early life with my mother: his discharge from the army in August 1945; a few identification certificates from his years before the war working for the Farm Security Administration; my mother's brief holograph will, witnessed by a hospital nurse, dated November 1958, two weeks before she died; three prints of her wedding portrait from 1943; and the scrapbook she had begun to make of their courtship. Titled "Our Hearts Were Young and Gay," the fat book's black pages begin the story of their life densely: photographs tipped in with black corner mounts, letters clipped from magazines and glued in separately to spell out the places and pleasures of their first months together. Soon the pages thin. All that remains on some are the empty corner mounts. Most of the book is blank. Like much of the rest of what survived in that cardboard produce carton, the scrapbook is finally just a fragment.

But packed in the bottom, squeezed in beneath the portraits and the scrapbook and the certificates, were bundles of letters and cables he sent to her in San Francisco between 1942 and 1943 while he was stationed in New Guinea. One hundred and ninety-nine of them. Some record the tedium of his days; none mentions danger. Mostly they express longing. Again and again, they return to the sweet memory of the night he proposed to her at Cedars and they ate cold hamburgers at midnight to celebrate. In the last rush of the letters, when he has been unexpectedly reprieved and is suddenly on his way home—his cables overtaking the letters as he races across the ocean: "On my way, on my way!"—I see them as I never saw them when they were alive, swinging each other across a Market Street dance floor, blushing with reckless hope.

They were young in 1943, just married, in the middle of World War II in San Francisco. My father was home safe from combat but had been reassigned to an air corps that might still fly him back into war. My mother had been for a while in the convent of the Sisters of Mercy in Burlingame, but her health had forced her to leave. They had no money and no prospects of any, and every day must have seemed uncertain to them.

But in the middle of the Latin Mass—at Star of the Sea

Church out on Geary Street—the priest would intone "Sursum Corda," and they would respond with the rest of the congregation, "Habemus ad Dominum."

"Let us lift up our hearts."

"We have lifted them up to the Lord."

For their first Christmas my mother gave my father a gold ring inscribed on the back with that wonderful exhortation: "Sursum Corda."

Where did she get such recklessness? What grace touched her spirit? Sudden, impulsive, with a hope that was positive and insistent, that rushed out of her smiling face. Where did it come from?

She must have felt death gaining on her. She could smell the sickness oozing out of her pores. She pulled me aside in the kitchen on Reinhardt Drive one night when I was ten or eleven years old to ask me to smell her: was she all right for her guests? Some days my brother and sister and I would make her so frustrated she would threaten us helplessly with what our father would do when he came home. Some days she would punish us herself. One afternoon she jerked me by the wrist straight to the boxwood shrub at the edge of the lawn beneath their bedroom window. Off came the branch, and then the twigs and leaves, and then she thrashed me across the calves with the switch until I cried out in mock pain. I remember days when she was so exhausted or upset she shut herself into her bedroom, lay in the gloom of eucalyptus shade, and wept.

Perhaps the hope she felt in 1943 simply shriveled up and by the time I was old enough to notice had disappeared. But I think not. The morning of her funeral Mass, though it was November, the sun shone like spring, and St. Lawrence O'Toole's church was packed with her relatives and friends. As they tried clumsily to say something comforting to me, I could see in their faces their own grief. Later, as they talked to me of her, they all said the same thing: she was so bright and happy, she was a little flower, she danced and she laughed.

Her impulses were not prudent or reasonable. One Saturday night, without checking the schedules or the fares, she called a neighbor friend to propose that the two of them catch a train to New York to meet her uncle from Ireland. "Let's just go," she said to Evelyn Tuschon (Evelyn told me this years later), "let's just do it." They did not go. Maybe neither of them ever really believed they could. But it cheered Evelyn to be asked, to pick up the phone on a Saturday night and hear Sheila's gay, reckless voice.

I have a photograph of her face that captures for me something of what they must have heard in her voice. Her auburn hair is brushed up into a wave off her forehead. High cheekbones, freckles, eyes squinting in the sun, and a huge smile full of bright teeth. It is a face I remember only vaguely from my childhood, though I have kept the picture with me ever since she died. My father, her brothers and sisters, their friends, all loved the fragile gaiety of her smiling face. She raised their spirits.

I do not know how to name this thing. I find myself using different words for it—hope, brightness, gaiety, desire. I do not know where it came from, but it is as mysterious as grace. Wherever, it must have been flickering, uncertain, flooding through her on some days, gone without a trace on others. Through the landing window of our house these days (I am now older than she was when she died), I sometimes catch the morning sun refracted by lilac blossoms against the brick wall across our yard. The light is so sweet and soft that it purifies for me all the promise of the day. It seems even to purify me.

But some mornings I am unable to see anything out that window except worn dirt and cracked paint and a broken drain spout at the corner of the garage.

Asked how I keep up my hope for teaching, some days all I can think to say is, "What hope?" But some days I think this: I come out of class, shouting greetings to everyone, stopping fellow teachers to tell them how astonishing it is that we are actually getting paid for this work. I grab someone's arm walking down the steps of Young Hall into a sea of students in the morning sun—everyone seems to me to be laughing, on their way to coffee or a late breakfast in the student union—I grab him to say that the students in my class just now thrilled me. At the end of class, some of them read their writing aloud to one another. It was daring stuff because the students are all new and self-conscious, and they hardly know each other. But it was full of their minds at work, one girl reading aloud about her fight with bulimia, another changing her mind in midsentence to say that what she had just been writing was nonsense, a third calling out across the room that he too had such a falling out with his best friend. My friend looks at me quizzically, shakes his head. "They can't read," he says. "They don't know what school is about." I ride over his objection, squeeze his arm again, say, "They were wonderful," and am off.

I find a place in a far, quiet corner of McConnell Library to reread *To the Lighthouse*. I come upon a passage that overwhelms me with such sympathy and love that I try to share it later in class. I take only a moment.

"Listen," I say, "you know the third floor, the mahogany carrels back against the yellow wall in the corner, back behind the stacks? I was sitting there this afternoon—hiding away from my office and phone—amazed by this book we're reading. I was trying to take notes, to remind myself of the shape and sequence of the book, trying to get organized for this class, and I couldn't do it. The book absorbed me.

"Listen: Lily Briscoe's standing on the lawn outside the Ramsays' summer house on an island off the coast of England. She's trying to paint a landscape. But while she paints she thinks about everything, so the subject of her painting becomes the landscape of all their lives—the house, time, Mrs. Ramsay, children, failure, loneliness, and in the center of it all, the lighthouse—all of them linked in her heart. Listen—you remember this part?—

What was it then? What did it mean? Could things thrust their hands up and grip one; could the blade cut; the fist grasp? Was there no safety? No learning by heart of the ways of the world? No guide, no shelter, but all was miracle, and leaping from the pinnacle of a tower into the air? Could it be, even for elderly people, that this was life?—startling, unexpected, unknown? For one moment she felt that if they both [she and old Mr. Carmichael] got up, here, now on the lawn, and demanded an explanation, why was it so short, why was it so inexplicable, said it with violence, as two fully equipped human beings from whom nothing could be hid might speak, then, beauty would roll itself up; the space would fill; those empty flourishes would form into a shape; if they shouted loud enough Mrs. Ramsay would return. "Mrs. Ramsay!" she said aloud, "Mrs. Ramsay!" The tears ran down her face.

Even if the students do not remember, even if they look blankly at me, wondering, I am undeterred. I tell them that for a moment I felt like Lily Briscoe. I almost called out in the library. The tears ran down my face.

I mean it as a gift.

Some days I am simply moved by the wonder of learning, by the beauty of it. Everywhere in school, we teachers and students are coming to know and understand. It takes different shapes; sometimes it looks like a miracle, sometimes an achievement. A girl in Margaret Grant's third-grade class in Missoula, Montana, is painstakingly writing out a line of a Halloween poem she is composing. A video camera is watching over her shoulder. She writes, "A SCARY SIGT ON HALLOWEEN NIG . . ."—and then the camera captures it, her recognition of the similarity of "sight" and "night" and of her having left the "h" out of "sight." She leaves the "nig" incomplete until she goes back to erase and correct "sigt."

One afternoon my eighteen-year-old son, Kevin, phoned me at work to tell me what he was thinking about a history paper he had to write on John Winthrop. This son for whom school had been about 85 percent wasted time surprised me in my office with a progress report. He had been to the library, he told me, and he thought he was figuring out what Winthrop meant by his idea that the Puritan colony could be a city on a hill. Kevin was beginning to understand why it failed. Not failed, exactly, but changed. In the very process of putting the idea into practice, Kevin said, Winthrop changed it and doomed it to failure.

I was silent on my end of the line, listening. I know almost nothing about Winthrop and the Puritan colonies. But I knew the impatience of Kevin's voice, and I could hear and feel the thrill of his mind at work.

In an upper-division undergraduate course in the literature of the English eighteenth century, a student wrote a paper about one feature of a single line from Samuel Johnson's poem "The Vanity of Human Wishes." The line occurs at the end of a two-couplet sentence describing the folly of praying for a long life:

> Enlarge my life with multitude of days,
> In health, in sickness, thus the suppliant prays;
> Hides from himself his state, and shuns to know,
> That life protracted is protracted woe.

A music major and a member of the university chorus, the student saw in the chiasmus of that last line a musical form. Her response: to compose a double crab canon as a musical setting for Johnson's poetic verse.

That is putting it too simply. The double crab canon was not merely a convenient musical form. Frequently employed by Bach, the canon, the crab canon, and the double crab canon were forms contemporary with Johnson. Furthermore, the crab canon is an *exact* analogue of chiasmus: the second half of its melodic line exactly mirrors the first. In poetry, that mirroring can be merely decorative, but in Johnson's line, the mirroring creates a deeper, more resonant meaning. In the crab canon, the mirroring can be merely a clever puzzle, but at its best it yields a richer and more complicated harmony.

More. The canon is often a verbal form, so its closeness to poetry made it a particularly appropriate choice. Though many lines of poetry have served as the inspiration for great instrumental musical compositions, the canon (especially one sung a capella) embodies the dynamic of chiasmus with particular efficiency.

More still. A canon is a round. One voice begins, then another. A crab canon is a round with a reversible melodic line. A double crab canon doubles the complications: it is two rounds with two different texts, each with reversible melodic lines, each sung simultaneously, each harmonizing with the other. Because of the structure of Johnson's line—it is simply a noun clause; the sentence of which it is the end begins in the preceding couplet—the student decided she needed more than a single crab canon to convey the whole meaning of Johnson's last line. So, with appropriate mathematical symmetry, she gave the four lines of Johnson's couplets the four voices of a double crab canon.

Listen. The first voice sings: "Enlarge my life with multitude of days." Then the second voice begins: "Protracted life." The third voice begins before the second ends, by repeating the line of the first: "Enlarge my life . . ." Finally, the fourth voice enters: "Protracted woe." And then the whole four lines are repeated, different voices singing different texts. But because a double crab canon is a round, the simultaneous voices gradually peel away from each other, until at the very end there is only one voice left, and its text, unencumbered, undiluted, is the line toward which Johnson and the student in my class have been working all along: "that life protracted is protracted woe."

When she presented the paper, she added a title page on musical composition paper that linked their names:

The Vanity of Human Wishes / a double crab canon / by / Cathy M. Barrow / on a text from / a poem / by / Samuel Johnson / © [Copyright] 1985 by CMBarrow.

She included as well a cassette tape on which she and three friends had sung the music she had made.

It is an exhilarating story on a melancholy text. No wonder she put her name to it. This was achievement so far beyond the expectations of my modest assignment that it gave me a new sense of what learning in school might be.

Sheila was from Ireland, grew up there, came over with her elderly father when she was a teenager, the last of her family to come to America. Her uncle, Bartholomew Kevany, was the pastor of Our Lady of Lourdes parish down on the edge of Lake Merritt in Oakland. We kids called him "Bayo." It was he who helped her and my father get established in Oakland. It was his huge polished DeSoto that parked on Reinhardt Drive outside our house. It was his cigar ash sprinkled on the white linen tablecloth when I got up before my mother on Saturday mornings, his cigar smell that suffused the rooms like incense. Our home and family must have been a refuge for him. He came often for dinner, dignified in his black suit and Roman collar and white hair. I never saw him loosen that collar, though I am sure he did. He stayed late, telling story after story over brandy. My father and he fished together in the foothills of the

Sierras, and when I was in the eighth grade—during my mother's last illness—Bayo took my father and me with him on a trip to the Ahwahnee Hotel in Yosemite Valley. In 1957, in celebration of the golden jubilee of his ordination to the priesthood, his parishioners at Our Lady of Lourdes sent him on a trip home to Ireland. It was the idea to meet his ship in New York that prompted Sheila to call Evelyn Tuschon and propose that they welcome him back. Fortunately, she did not live to see his mind fail him in the pulpit, to see him lose his way during Mass and walk off the altar in confusion.

For all the childhood I can remember with her, my mother wanted me to be a priest. I never felt that desire of hers as a pressure on me, though I now know that it certainly was. When St. Lawrence O'Toole's School devoted a week one year to vocations, I remember making a poster of a faceless priest, his back to the congregation, elevating the consecrated host during the Mass. I took it for granted that as soon as elementary school was over I would enter the seminary, as my great uncle had when he was a boy in Ireland. It was a rich and comfortable priesthood I imagined—vestments, DeSotos, cigars and black suits, no darned socks, no stains on my cassock from vomit or blood.

After four years I left the seminary, easily, and have never regretted the decision. I gave up being a priest and chose instead to become a teacher. I suppose that if my mother had lived, I would have found leaving more difficult. I suppose I would have felt that I was betraying her. But I know that the vocation of my childhood was a boy's imagining. Surrounded by rosaries and novenas and 6:30 Masses on weekday mornings as I was, my wanting to be a priest was no different from another boy's wanting to be a fireman.

It was also a mother's imagining. Though I can guess about the sources of her wish—herself in the convent until sickness forced her out, her uncle a priest, her niece a nun, her nephew already in the seminary, and the sense in Irish families that an eldest son's ordination was a special blessing from God—I can only guess. I cannot ask her why she wanted me to become a priest, and the voice with which she urged me to do so has faded.

163

Though I have kept all these years the photograph of her smiling face—it was taken on her wedding day in front of Our Lady of Lourdes Church—I had forgotten the lilt of her voice until my father gave me the ring she had given him. Then at once it all came back—his hands, the Bay Bridge lights, cigar smoke, standing under the backyard eucalyptus trees after her funeral, the quickness of her laugh, the brightness of her extravagant desire. "Let us lift up our hearts." For desire is what it was—not just for herself, or for my father, or for me; not just for health, or peace of mind, or laughter. "She could dance," my father told me, recalling their first dates on Thursday nights at a hall on the corner of VanNess and Market Streets in wartime San Francisco. "Dance. You should have seen her . . ." He paused, looked down at his old hands folded lightly on the table in our Radford breakfast room. "Oh . . . she was a marvelous dancer."

For our twentieth wedding anniversary, Susie gave me a gold signet ring specially cut to match the one I lost. She had the back engraved with "Sursum Corda," and thereby linked us all—her and me, Norma, my father, and Sheila.

I run my thumb along its band and imagine my mother's face, picture her red skirt flaring as she danced. I wish I had seen her. I wish I could remember more. But among my few distinct memories is this: when I was in the fifth grade, I became an altar boy, and took my turn serving at the early weekday Mass. I do not remember her waking me in the room where I slept with my brother or slipping out of the house while it was still dark. I must have been so sleepy that the ride down Carson to High Street and around to the back of the church passed in a blur lit only by the dim round panel lights on the dashboard. But when Mass was over and I had hung up my cassock and surplice in the sacristy, I stepped out the side door into the sun. And there was my mother waiting in the green Plymouth with the driver's door open. She motioned me in. I climbed up on her lap, my hands near the top of the steering wheel, and the two of us drove back up the hill to home.

14

Joy

I URGE NEW teachers of Freshman English to teach with joy, then make entries like this in my journal:

> I have a strange feeling of distance from this class, as if I've never really gotten involved with them. As if from a distance, preoccupied with other stuff, I've never really committed myself to these folks. They seem to be just floating out there—writing their weakly essays (weakly—weekly) dutifully but not really getting in tune with what I mean or seeing what it is that I want them to do or coming to find it valuable.

I prepare class, hoping for intellectual excitement, and the hour fizzles by. Students attend (most of them), awake (except for one in the front row), do exactly what I ask—write when I assign writing, discuss when I suggest discussion. Exactly. They take me literally, think I'm giving them instructions. Our exchanges are cordial and lifeless, as if someone had switched the current off.

This is not joy I feel.

In a eulogy for Henri Peyre, former president of the Modern Language Association, professor Victor Brombert recently wrote,

> We loved him, as entire generations of students have loved him—not a little awed by him, not a little afraid to be teased by him, yet also enjoying that teasing with some pride. What he meant to us was first and foremost the joy of the classroom: that fervor, that knowledge, that scope, those resplendent digressions, those feasts

165

of ideas, and that voice, that sunny voice of his. We wondered and marveled. To those of us who later followed him in the teaching profession it was the first revelation of what we learned over and over to be true—that no book we write, no book review we receive, no honor bestowed on us can equal the elation, the thrill of seeing an entire class come alive with the excitement of ideas, of seeing the signs of intelligent response to what is clearly perceived as a privileged moment. We would be disconsolate if we were to lose that joy.

Is joy something we can keep or lose? The word keeps coming back to us as we try to define the gift that teaching sometimes seems. But we are hard pressed to say what we mean.

One of Sandra Boynton's cartoons decorates little 3M Post-it pads of notepaper. It is reproduced in educational book catalogues and adorns coffee mugs on teachers' shelves. It shows a row of school desks in which the pupils (a wonderful assortment of loveable animals) are deployed in zany poses. Not one of them is doing schoolwork. All are absorbed in being intractable. The cat is balancing on one foot on the offended turkey's desk. The lamb is turned around in his seat and, with the dog, who is under the lamb's chair, is watching intently the cat's performance. The pig is asleep, even through this. The teacher, at his desk in the front of the room, has given up and is looking at us. The caption of the cartoon reads, "The little joys of teaching are without number."

This cartoon delights teachers. Every one of us has felt the helpless exasperation of Boynton's wide-eyed owl-teacher. We all have had moments of sheer appreciation for the amazing range and resourcefulness of our students, especially when it comes to avoiding work or confounding our lessons. The "little" in the caption echoes our affection for schoolchildren (of all ages).

But the deeper source of delight in the cartoon is that it renders comic our desperation. It makes light of our dismay. The joys of teaching, the cartoon says, are little. They are without number not only because there are so many, but because there are so few. We cannot count them. We cannot count *on* them. This is a cartoon less about joy than about getting on, about making do. Joy resists definition.

Joy

The little joys of teaching are without number

But second-grade teacher Marcia Umland, from Albany, California, comes closer to identifying the joy of teaching than anyone else I have heard. Interviewed in Ken Macrorie's *Twenty Teachers*, Umland describes her students with a voice animated by respect and wonder. She encourages children to write notes to her, to each other, to the janitor and the school secretary, and to themselves. When they write stories, she confers with them and urges them to revise. She invites them to help her compose her written reports of their work and behavior, and when conflicts among children arise, she asks them to talk out possible solutions among themselves. Hers is a classroom in which oranges and witches, broken lockers and sandwiches are the stuff of stories and pictures to be exchanged and admired. It is exhausting work but motivated by an invigorating principle: "Lately I've realized," she says, "that in setting up a classroom at last I've given myself permission to form a society I'd like to live in."

I misread her at first. I thought she meant she had succeeded, that she had in fact formed such a society. Her story is so packed with moments of delight—the second-graders' calling their block structure a hotel, not just a tower; one girl's refusing to share her writing about her bad day on the reasonable ground that it was hers and nobody else's—that it was easy for me to conclude that Umland had solved the puzzle of school. I wanted her to have solved it (never mind the envy I knew I

167

would also feel). When Macrorie says to her, "I wish I had been in your class when I was a kid," I agree. When Umland—who hated school when she was young—says, "I wish I had, too," it is easy for me to imagine that here is the classroom of my dreams.

But things are more complicated than they seem. And Umland is more acutely honest than I knew. Always her teaching is different; some years it doesn't work at all. "One class may take longer to learn to work with me instead of against me than another. In my present class it may be spring before we'll be the kind of class I'd like to be in." In other words, it may *never* be that kind of class. The classroom she describes to Macrorie is in fact *no* classroom, not even her own. It is made up of fragments of her portrait of herself—her work in public schools, private schools, as a substitute, running a day-care nursery school, teaching second and third grade.

It is less her class I want to be in than her presence. I want to give her my stories to read. I want to hear her laughter. I want to ask her help in thinking about my teaching. She gives herself permission. I want to learn from her to give myself permission, too. Her account is an image of her desire. The classroom she and Macrorie and I all want to be in is the classroom implicit in her joy.

C. S. Lewis describes this characteristic of joy in his spiritual autobiography:

> The form of the desired is in the desire. It is the object which makes the desire harsh or sweet, coarse or choice, "high" or "low." It is the object that makes the desire itself desirable or hateful. . . . Joy itself, considered simply as an event in my own mind, turned out to be of no value at all. All the value lay in that of which Joy was the desiring.

So, in the end, what happens in Umland's class is less important than what she wants to happen. It is the difference between looking back and looking forward, between the finished and the potential. I thought she was saying that she had made the society she wanted to live in. What she is saying in fact is that she allows herself to try.

I write in my journal:

I don't know how to transform this class. I have this feeling that what I'm doing in here needs to be transformed. That it needs to be more serious, more valuable, more pervasively important to their thinking and experience than school is.
   I want to ask you [them?] a question: What would school have to be, what would this class have to be, for you to fight its cancellation?
   I can't ask them that question. They can't imagine it, for one thing, and for another, why does school have to create that kind of response? There are a lot of things that folks can find valuable that they wouldn't fight for. . . .
   Well, this is just a snarl of thought.
   I better stop.

I was unable to work out the puzzle of that entry when I ran into Jana Gelderman on the stairs in Young Hall. Jana had been a student in one of my Freshman English classes two years before; she was on her way to France for the second semester of her junior year. We walked out of the building together.
   "How're your classes?" she asked.
   "OK," I said. "But I can't quite shake the feeling that we're not really in touch with each other. They do their work. I read and grade it. But there's no contact; it's as if we're in a sterile environment, all wearing masks and gloves."
   Jana did not even pause, "Have you talked with them about it?"
   Well, no, I hadn't. Every time I considered it, my words sounded phoney, histrionic: What would make you willing to fight for this class? I imagined myself exhorting them with sentiment: Joy. That's what I want for us in here. Do you understand? Joy.
   No, I had not talked with them about it, but Jana's comment made me realize I had not talked with them very much at all, even about their writing. Talked with them. Not just given them assignments or models or rules or grades. Had not read to them, had not let them see what I valued in what they were doing. There was much to value.

Thanks to Jana's frankness, I looked at the potential in my students' work. Suddenly I saw them differently. I typed up pieces of their work, photocopied them for everyone in class, read them aloud, and talked about them.

In her journal, Sharon Mays wrote:

Nov 2 Friday

What I think is strong in my draft for this week is that I have made who I am speaking too clear. Thinking back though I don't know that the point would be clear to anyone else but me. It does tell that I was close to my sister and I miss those times now that were older and I'm in college. So I could be telling her that I miss those times. I like this paper because I was able to sit down and let the words flow. When I was trying to think up a topic my roommate helped me. I just started telling her things my sister and I did when I was little. She said there's your topic. Because I couldn't stop remembering all the things we had done.

This was school, but Sharon could not stop remembering what mattered to her.

The first paragraph of one of Jeanette Webley's essays began with the following scene:

My mother and father looked so pleased standing in the crowd. Everyone was listening to me give my speech of what I have done in my life and what I plan to do in the future. The sun was beating down on my back and in the background of my speech there was a quartet playing. My speech was addressed to the Daughters of the American Revolution. Thanking them for giving me the honor of receiving the good citizenship award from my school.

Not only was Jeanette proud of herself, but in her rendering of the whole feeling of that moment—when "the sun was beating down on my back and in the background of my speech there was a quartet playing"—yes, there was, there was, and it is still playing—she suggests that the audience shared her feeling, that honor was in the very air itself.

Michelle Garrett wrote about grief:

The endless time spent at the hospital waiting for a change in grandad's condition was my unhappiest. I looked in the halls and the waiting room. Everyone had someone to lean on. Pairs of relatives slowly walked in and out of the blue Intensive Care doors. I saw my sister and her boyfriend outside the special room. She crying as he held her. I hated them both. I had no tears as I exited. Why did she claim the right to cry? She was no better than I yet her tears showed she was human—me the cold rock.

The essay of which that is a part is at once unadorned and sophisticated. It is not about her but about her cousin, not about her own grief but about his. She sees him at a funeral, withdrawn, inconsolable, and is reminded of her own lonely sorrow. As such, it reanimates its own clichés: the person who could be a "cold rock" stands silent, watching her cousin, understanding. By means of concrete facts and spare statement, Michelle defines both the boy's feeling and her own. The doors of the Intensive Care ward are blue. Her sister is crying in her boyfriend's arms; Michelle hates them both. This is an astonishing effect—to use her hatred to convey her sympathy. Her cousin is standing alone. Michelle is standing nearby, waiting for him, love welling up in her words.

Chip Flood sat in the front of the classroom, against the wall, just inside the door. He wore jeans and most days a T-shirt, and he never took off his black-billed Allis-Chalmers cap. He came almost every day to class, but he did not say one word aloud during the entire semester. Suddenly, in the middle of the term, he wrote this journal entry. I went over to him and whispered, "Chip, can I use your journal entry with the class?" He said, "Sure," and shrugged.

I really considered myself as an under par writer. I've had this problem ever since I was in the elementary school. Teachers have had numerous talks to me about my papers but nothing seemed to help. The problem arose when I was in the 4th grade. At the time I was a active member in the 4-H club and we had to do so many projects each year to stay in the club. One of my planned projects for that particular year was to do a speech. It could be on anything. Here it was, the day of the speeches and I had completely forgotten all about it! All my friends were harassing me telling me if I didn't do one I would be kicked out of the club! I soon became very upset and even asked to go to the library so I could maybe write something for my speech. I ended up with a short speech on "Cats." It was the laughing stock of the year that gave me a complex for the rest of my live.

The next day the class met he was absent. Another student spoke up, "You remember that journal you read of Chip's the other day? You know, you could sort of tell that something like that had happened to him once." Twenty-three students in the class. They don't know each other, come from different backgrounds, different worlds. A student like Chip keeps absolutely to himself. But in spite of his reticence, his journal so touched that girl that it made her wish to declare it aloud. I wish he had been there to hear it.

Like Chip, Missy Harris was thinking about her own experience as a writer in the following journal entry:

> I had never considered myself a good writer until my Junior year. I was on the Prom Committee and we were searching for a poem for Prom. I was depressed because my boyfriend and I had broken up 2 months before Prom. I sat down and wrote a silly poem & gave it to the committee. They unanimously decided to use it. I finally got a date and was told I had to read my poem to the crowd on prom night & then they would play the theme song. I was so nervous that night that I couldn't enjoy the first 1/2 of the dance. When the time came I went to the stage & stood looking at the sea of faces below me, half of them drunk. I knew I was going to be laughed off the stage. I started reading in a shaky voice but all I heard was silence. I read on for what seems like an eternity until I reached the end. I stopped, looked up and saw every girl crying. There was silence for a minute then a deadening roar of applause and shouts. I was so stunned I almost fainting. As I came off the stage my ex-boyfriend came up to me, put his arm around me & said, "I'm proud of you kid!" I calmly looked at him and said "Get your slimy hands off me you bastard" and walked off leaving him stunned.

When I read that last line, the class roared their appreciation. Never mind that it was eight o'clock in the morning; they cheered for Missy. The way she captures that patronizing boyfriend: "I'm proud of you, kid." The way she sets up their split:

he didn't take her to the dance; she had to get a date with somebody else. The way she comes straight back at him, fiery. The prom poem was not only the best piece of writing she had ever done; it got her feeling so good about herself that she just told the guy, "Get out of my life. What are you doing here with your hands on me?"

When things calmed down, someone in class asked, "You mean you can say *that*? I didn't know you could say *that*."

All these bits of writing from students in a single class sparkle with wit, humor, wisdom, insight. In each, the writers rendered public a private memory grounded in details that are pointed and purposeful. Not one of them is flawless, but each is rich with potential. What they created for me—in a semester when I wrote to myself that my class was drifting through time—was an image of surprising power. Students have within themselves a complex sense of the world and deep reservoirs of thought and feeling. Sometimes they cannot stop remembering.

Sometimes we teachers forget. Swamped by piles of papers, surrounded by phantoms of laziness and listlessness, boredom and insolence, it's easy to forget the latent power of students and the potential of our work together. Again and again, I have forgotten. But to remember our potential as teachers and students is to conceive of a society in which we would like to live. It is to imagine a school of which this particular classroom (*any* classroom) is just a draft. To recover faith in students—to talk with them, as Jana suggested I should, to look at their work with fresh eyes—is to believe again in oneself as a teacher and in a relationship between teachers and students in which both learn and grow. It is to permit oneself desire and joy.

You may say, "This is maudlin. Let's see how successful you are. Show us your good works. You have to teach within the institution of school, so grades and requirements and syllabi are a must. You can't just dispense with report cards and teaching evaluations. Quit pretending. The puzzle of school won't be solved by a wave of your heart."

Which is to claim that joy comes only after the fact. I want to argue that it can come before.

In *Fallible Man*, Paul Ricoeur elaborates a description of

the fragility of human beings. According to Ricoeur, our weakness is ontological, in our very being. We are mixed, animal and angelic. We stand between God and nothingness, our soul itself a striving toward being. Knowing our own incompleteness, our hearts are restless. Our feelings resist finite satisfaction. They are merely the promise of happiness, never the fulfillment of happiness itself. In such a state, the two fundamental human feelings are anguish and joy. Anguish at the recognition that we lack what we desire most (and are therefore distant from it). Joy at the recognition that in our very desire we partake of what we lack (and are therefore linked to it in love).

But what is that pure, innocent, complete state of being toward which we yearn? Ricoeur does not say. Because we are essentially fallen, we cannot say what the *un*-fallen might be. But joy provides us with a glimmer of it. By an act of imagination, joy transcends the fallible limits of our incomplete being. It breaks, Ricoeur says, the prestige of fact. It gives us a glimpse not only of what is possible (never mind our daily experience of limit) but of what is essential.

Ricoeur's analysis of our humanity helps explain why teachers like Marcia Umland, with a class still working against her, manage to hang on to their dream. It helps explain why discerning the power in student work gives me such pleasure and hope. When we teach and learn with joy, we invent in our imaginations the school that could be.

Mike sat in the back of that same class—with Sharon May and Jeanette Webley, with Michelle and Chip—hid back there as long as he could. Hardly said anything. Thought himself a lousy student. Thought himself incapable of doing much that was successful at all. Came to Radford. Wanted to go to the University of Virginia, but did not have strong enough high school grades or recommendations. Perked up for one paper that he decided to write about the failures of the UVa basketball coach (Mike's family lived in Charlottesville, so he knew a lot about the UVa basketball program and its recent history). But even then he remained quiet and undemonstrative. The thing he liked most was rock and roll and the band of guys back home that he used to play with (he played the drums, didn't sing; as in class, he kept himself as quiet as possible).

He did not talk at all about this essay, with me or with any-one else so far as I know. Nevertheless, it turned out more im-portant to him than either basketball or rock and roll. He did not think he was a writer. He had never written anything twice in his life. Then he wrote this one essay, letting it grow through a series of versions, coming back to it again and again.

Watch his mind move through a journal entry:

> Hey all of you people. Where are you going to go on your vaca-tion this year? Sure California and Florida are very attractive. But have you ever considered the state of Maine to spend a relaxing couple of weeks. They don't call Maine the Vacationland for nothing.
>
> The State is a switch from the busy, hected, and crowded usual vacation spots. You don't have world famous places that can ruin a vacation. . . . You can enjoy a day at the coast and visit famous Bar Harbor. While at the coast you can enjoy fishing flounder and digging clams. To top it off, feast on the world's best lobsters.
>
> Maine is a heaven for campers. Maine has over 3,500 lakes to which to choose from. Enjoy camping / / / / / / / / hiking, go by a stream, blueberries,
>
> > wildlife
> > canoeing
> > fishing

Unlike a typical journal entry, in which Mike talked to him-self or to me about what or how he was doing in his work, this entry is already on its way to becoming a draft of an essay. It al-ready has a provisional audience, and it is already exploring the benefits of a Maine vacation. It ends with a list of items Mike seems to want to pursue, and in fact when he developed this en-try into a full draft, these last items became the center of his at-tention. Here is part of that first draft:

> I can remember as a little boy the urge to go to Maine. The urge was one of ———. I remember crying once because our trip to Maine was canceled. When my parents tell me that were going to Maine or there sending us I just get excstatic. On the eve before I never go to sleep because I'm too exciting. The 14 hour car trip or the three hour plane trips always seem to take forever.

175

When I get there I just want to jump straight in the boat. My grandparents had a house on Chemo Pond up until two years ago. Chemo is surrounded by thick forests of great pines and evergreens.

The highlight of my time is Maine is to go fishing. [crossed out: Before my grandfather would have to] I drove my grandfather crazy because I wanted to fish everyday. I was too young to drive the boat than. We'd go out and I have a great time even if we didn't catch bass.

This past year made me more appreciative. I got up around 5:00 and drove over to Chemo. Everything was silent . . .

Mike's vision of his subject was being refined as he moved from the journal to this draft. In the journal, he began: Hey, you guys. Let me tell you about a great vacation spot . . . , as if he were working up an informal brochure for a travel agency. That approach did not work—at least Mike left it unfinished—but already it is clear to us that he knows and likes a lot about Maine. The item at the very bottom of his journal list was "fishing." It was as if he stopped there, saw that it could be his subject, and then wrote his way toward it in this draft. "The highlight of my time in Maine is to go fishing."

Something else happened, too. His grandparents' house on Chemo Pond, the way he drove his grandfather crazy wanting to fish every day, and his last summer there—when all these coalesced for him, he wrote still another draft. This is how it begins:

The Maine morning was beautiful. Across the lake, the sun balanced on the peak of Chick Hill. It shot beams of light onto the clouds which turned them fire orange. The mountains reflected clearly off the mirror-like water. Everything was still and silent. The singing Chickadees indicated that there was life after all on Chemo Pond. A slight southeast breeze blew but it wasn't forceful enough to shake the limbs of the towering evergreens. The air was cool and crisp which woke me up.

I loaded the boat with all the necessities: rod, tackle box, life seat, and some snacks. Instead of starting the motor at the dock, I paddled out some distance to avoid waking up my grandparents. I cranked up the motor and was on my way to my favorite shoreline. I was excited, not only because of the challenging fishing that awaited, but because I was at my favorite place in the world. . . .

Mike would never call himself a writer, but his work here speaks for itself. He got lots of words down, followed where they led, and then went back and cut—cut the past, his parents, vacationland, cut his crying because they canceled their visit, cut the car ride and the plane trip—until all that was left was the morning sun on Chick Hill.

After he had written it, we finally talked. It was our only conversation of the semester. Even then he spoke hesitantly, as he still did years later when I ran into him in a bicycle repair shop. He had a bike frame up on the rack, his fingers concentrating on the derailleur he was installing. I waited through long pauses. That was his way. If you did not know any better, you would think he was not listening. That he was indifferent, careless, distant. But, yes, he remembered the paper about fishing, he said. When he glanced up at me, I saw the same pride and gladness he had felt when he finished it.

The essay on Chemo Pond was the purest statement he had ever made about the purest pleasure he had ever known.

15

Commencement

TERESA SIMPSON. Gaby Wade. Philip Arca. Jana Gelderman. John Wilson. They stand applauding as we march toward the rows of chairs reserved for us on Muse lawn in front of the library. Malia Haley holds her hat with one bare arm and jumps up with her other waving, the sleeves of her graduation robe flapping. "Dr. Murphy. Dr. MURPHY. Hiiii, Dr. Murphy!" I grab for her outstretched hand, press it with both of my own, then am carried away from her by the procession. On both sides of the grassy aisle, students I know are banked, waiting, some standing on their chairs, students I knew but whose names I cannot now remember. Then, suddenly, a name returns effortlessly: "Gerry! Congratulations." Gerry says quickly, "I'd like you to meet my parents." I say, "Sure. I'll look for you afterwards by the fountain." "Pomp and Circumstance" keeps us moving toward our seats, and I hum as we march.

The sun shines reliably for college commencements in California; not so in Virginia. By the first week in May, summer rains have begun—morning showers, rainbows, triumphant thunderstorms in the afternoon, maple trees steaming at sunset. Saturated by rain, the campus lawns grow brilliantly green. Along the walks, lilac drips sweet purple in the moist air. The maintenance crews that unload and set up the rented chairs wait out downpours standing together in the backs of the truck trailers, smoking. When the rain is light, little more than mist, they keep on working, arranging the thousands of chairs in precisely fanned rows.

Commencement

Then, the morning of graduation, the president and his staff go into a caucus—Should we risk it? Should we move the ceremony to the convocation center (which means, because of limited seating, turning many people away)? It's only 7:30 now; by 11:00 will the rain have passed? Or will it have come? I admire their nerve. In all the years I have taught at Radford, graduation has been moved inside only once. But sometimes it has been so close a call that it has made even me giddy. Last year the rain held off until the very end. Then, the moment the ceremony was over, everyone—eighteen hundred graduates and upwards of another seven thousand family, friends, faculty, visitors—had to run for cover. The rain dropped for a solid half hour, turning the lawn in front of the library into a lake.

I am always ambivalent about graduation. For most students, this is it—the end of college, the end of school. I cannot suppress the feeling that for most of them it was not good enough, that we (they and their teachers both) were not good enough. I have the impression that some students should not be graduating yet. They do not seem to have the slightest sense of what education is or can be. But they have made it through the system—sixteen years or more—and their very success seems to me like failure. Other students go through graduation without having completed the last requirements, intending to finish up sometime during the summer. Their diploma envelopes are empty. In fact, all the graduates' are; the actual diplomas are sent home by mail. This fact seems emblematic to me: graduation is ceremony without substance.

I think that is why the faculty's presence is required. If it were not, I might not attend. I am not alone. Participation in graduation ceremonies is listed in our staff handbook: "Faculty members are expected to attend and participate in all commencements unless they have prior written approval of the President to be absent." A few of the faculty serve as ushers, keeping reserved seats empty and helping families and guests find places to sit or stand. As soon as everyone is in place, the ushers are free to leave. They usually do.

Still, the occasion seduces. Parents and grandparents carry lawn chairs across Fairfax Street on their way to the quad. A young woman in heels runs along the sidewalk, her gown bil-

179

lowing out behind her, one hand holding her bobby-pinned hat on her head. I do not have a mirror in my office, so I pause in front of the display case that lists the English department faculty names and offices and straighten my hood in the glass. Sun or not on graduation day, I am moved by it, and the feeling is a mixture of sadness, surprise, and the memory of hope.

I am amazed at how many of us there are, faculty and students. The faculty gather before graduation over beside Walker Hall, in full academic regalia. Black gowns, brown, blue, scarlet. Our hoods brilliant: white, yellow, aqua, pink, maroon, green, orange. Some of us have mortarboards on; a few wear no hats. I am one of the hatless ones. I do not look for mine until the morning of graduation, rummaging in the hall closet and on the cupboard shelf behind my hiking boots, and then, thankfully, I cannot find it. Some of us have the most wonderful hats—I would wear one of *those*—magenta berets and royal blue Renaissance caps from universities such as the Sorbonne and Genoa. Splendidly costumed (we hardly look like ourselves on the morning of graduation), we gather on the walks and the lawns. The space can barely contain us. We all say the same thing: "I didn't know the faculty had gotten so large." Then, in the distance, the university band starts to play, and we fall into a makeshift line.

When our column turns the corner of the walk near the fountain and begins to wind its way down the aisle among the waiting graduates, the sheer mass of them is stunning. Row after row, all in black, mortarboards decorated with adhesive tape ("Thanks, Mom!"—"KZP"—"Free at Last"), already into the pre-ceremony champagne, they go on forever. A sea of students. Where did they all come from? The handful I recognize only disorient me more: what class were they in? when? I try to be excited for them, glad. And I am. It is just that I cannot quite remember them.

The chaplain recites the invocation, the president welcomes everyone, the rector of the Board of Visitors urges graduates not to forget their alma mater (that is, particularly when they receive requests from the alumni office for donations), and the senior class speaker says that today is the first day of the rest of their lives. I half-listen. When we have an invited commencement speaker, I try to pay closer attention, and I always concentrate during the presentation of the teaching prizes. But then the deans of the different colleges announce their graduates, and different contingents of the audience start shouting, and the vice-president for academic affairs begins to call each of the thousands of names of graduating students, and all of this melts into an indistinguishable hum of background for my imagination.

On an ordinary day, the lawn is empty of chairs and guests. No temporary stage fronts the library steps. A bare-backed boy rides on a mountain bike from Reed to Heth, careening from side to side of the wide white walk. Two girls sit with their legs in the fountain pool. A fraternity gathered around a huge wooden wheel is collecting money at the start of a fund-raising walk to Richmond for the March of Dimes. The sophomore class is building a three-hundred-foot submarine sandwich outside Madison dormitory, their bid for some record. On the steps of Heth, a young man in a white shirt earnestly waves his Bible at a mixed crowd of curious and devout. A spray-painted sheet tied over the student union porch advertises an afternoon lecture called "Maximum Sex." Down near Young, three guys in peach and lemon shorts watch as a fourth lines up a long croquet shot.

My mind anachronizes the scene. Chris Davis is there, and the girl on the seashore who dropped out of college after five weeks. Gerhard, too, who was up with the crew on the Los Gatos reservoir at dawn. So are Sandra Miyoshi and Ms. E. Sanders—the student who thought I listened harder than any teacher she had ever known and the student who thought I did not listen at all. I remember myself as a student among them, making plans with my friends for the weekend at Santa Cruz, wondering how I was going to have time to finish my paper on *Huckleberry Finn* and *The Last of the Mohicans*. I see myself standing on the sidewalk talking with one of my professors about Wordsworth and feel again the ambivalence I had forgotten: *he* is far more interested in this than I am, I think; how can I get away?

This always happens to me at graduation: past and present coalesce. One year a distinguished guest speaker addressed us.

Plainclothes security guards were everywhere, mingling with parents, relatives, and friends gathered near the stage. I think they were trying to look inconspicuous in their seersucker suits, as if they were just friends of the family, but it was no good. Their eyes darted incessantly. They could not stand still. More of them hovered behind the stage, two on the library steps, another team up on the roof. I was watching them, so even though I tried to listen, I missed the speech.

But there was something else, a quiet droning, growing. A bumblebee? A car? The security men grew agitated. There, around the edge of the library roof, a single-engine plane appeared, its hum now a whine. It was flying over the campus, directly over the lawn. Arcing broadly. Buzzing the graduation. The curve of its trajectory a bright smile in the blue mid-morning sky. It flew lazily. It was in no hurry. It gave us all plenty of time to look up. The pitch of the plane's whine sank as it curved its way back over Reed Hall and out of sight.

Then it came round a second time. Buzz, whine, smile, message. Trailing behind on two cables, a long banner waved in silhouette: "I LOVE YOU, SARAH—CRAIG." It was terrific. The speaker's voice and the plane lulled me with their joint hum. Whoever Sarah and Craig were, I was delighted.

They reminded me of my own graduation from Santa Clara. The night before, the dorm prefects had locked me out of Nobili, the residence hall where I lived, so I spent it surreptitiously in Susie's apartment. I slept in my clothes on the couch in her living room. Early the next morning she woke me with a glass of fresh orange juice. I went back to my dorm to change, we met her parents and mine for breakfast, and then got to graduation late, racing in through the parking lot behind Varsi, holding our gowns up to keep ourselves from tripping. My young sister Tish brought us each a huge helium balloon—a deep blue one for Susie, blood red for me—the most fabulously beautiful balloons of my life—and we stood around in the Mission Gardens afterwards, holding them and each other. The sun shone that day, too. The gladness I felt was easy and inexpressibly clean.

Graduation felt real then. Today it feels like theater, an illusion of worn sets and old props still working its strange magic. All we need to be happy is to suspend our disbelief.

This year I was listening to the names being read, sipping ice water from the Styrofoam cup I had smuggled in within the bell sleeve of my robe and then balanced on the grass beneath my chair. One of my neighbors was commenting on a student of hers who had just been announced ("Summa cum laude," my friend said, "and as nice a person as you'd ever want to meet"). A colleague on the other side of me was reading a paperback novel. One faculty member at the end of the row in front of us was arguing with some nearby parents; he had brought a rainbow-colored golf umbrella to protect himself from the sun (or rain), but his umbrella was blocking their view and they were asking him to put it down.

It was the usual. Girls in lemon dresses pressing up to the stage steps to take pictures of their brothers or boyfriends. Pockets of family cheering crazily for their graduate when she walked across the stage ("Yaaaay, SHERRyyyy!!"). The hypnosis of names being read, one after the other, in a warm bath of laughter and murmuring talk.

Suddenly there was a scuffle. Arms flailing, black robe, shorts and a khaki shirt. No one actually punched anyone, I think. But by the time I could focus on what was happening, two members of the security staff had a student by the arms and had lifted him out of the line and up against the rope barrier to the side of the stage steps. A third attendant closed in then, and they had him in a pocket against the ropes. His gown was gone. He was wearing army surplus field shorts and a nondescript khaki shirt. Apparently, he had worn the gown up to the steps and then tried to slip out of it just as he started up to the stage. If so, it had been very close. He had almost made it.

I was absorbed. Gradually the guys holding him relaxed their grip. One of them reached down, picked up his gown, folded it loosely and handed it to him. The student balled it up and stuck it under his arm. So far as I could tell, he was not saying anything; they were doing all the talking. But no one was making any moves. They should not have let their guard slip. As soon as they did, he was under the rope and veering again toward the stairs. But he did not succeed this time either. They intercepted him at the stair rail. Once they got hold of him now, they did not let go; they walked him straight away, to wherever, to jail, I think someone said. I was disappointed.

I wished he had made it. All he wanted, apparently, was the freedom *not* to wear a robe as he graduated. But I was shocked by his daring and exhilarated by his single-mindedness. After the ceremony was over, I walked back to the stage alone. Wadded there on the lawn behind the rope—like all the other trash strewn among the chairs and across the quad, programs, Styrofoam cups, Hardee's bags—was the black nylon gown he had rented from the bookstore for the day.

His name was Michael (I forget his last name). He was a student in one of my classes. A nonconformist even then, he was always alone, sat in the front row with a canvas rucksack at his feet. Silent, watching me. He never disrupted class. On rare occasions he asked a question—harmless, a slight thing, some little bit of clarification he seemed to need—but never as simple as it appeared. His puzzling inquisitiveness would dismember the floor beneath us, piece by piece, as I looked down in wonder and the class looked up confused. Before he was done with me, I would have to try to reconstruct the whole intellectual tradition of the West.

Michael was not trying to be discourteous. He certainly did not mean to usurp class time. He was just as likely to wait afterwards and ask then. Patient, he was infinitely patient. If he had something else to do—it never seemed to occur to him that I had something else to do—it could wait. He did not speak quickly, just the reverse. His body would start to move, announcing an utterance that had not even begun forming. Then there would be an "Uh . . ." and something behind his eyes would brighten as the words started to collect. When I finally answered what he had asked, the periods at the ends of my sentences refused to stay put. He continued to watch fixedly, staring beyond me to the memory of the sentence I thought I had finished. Then my own period, as if bewitched by his concentration, would stretch into an ellipsis, and the conversation I thought was over would resume.

He was acute. Penetrating. His mind was unlike any others

I have encountered as a teacher. I do not think he was mad, as Lionel Trilling thought Tertan was. But he was surely out of place. He always sat in the same seat. He had no friends I ever saw. If we passed on campus he would not greet me, or, if I forced a hello, he would look at me startled, as if drawn out of some deep meditation. He wore the same clothes day in and day out, summer and winter, army surplus khaki field shorts or a pair of long trousers. He kept the field shorts in the bag with his books. Sometimes I saw him in town, riding an old battered one-speed bicycle with a wire basket for the rucksack over the front tire, his trousers cuff-clipped at his ankles.

School has few folks as stubborn as Michael, but it has plenty who, like him, are out of place. We are all out of place some days. We all look up and wonder how we got here. Our days together are filled with transactions that abort and with others that, though successful, seem mindless.

Visit a classroom. Go all the way back to first grade; the story is the same as it is in college. The classroom is full of tables each with four miniature chairs. On the rug, up near the chalkboard at the front of the room, the teacher is surrounded by twenty-three six-year-olds. The children are to kneel or sit cross-legged around her feet, but these are *little* children. They squirm and wiggle and talk and interrupt and have a great deal of difficulty settling down and staying settled ("Oh, boys and girls, I LOVE the way Priscilla is sitting so *STILL*. And Jason, Jason's sitting very nicely, too"). The teacher is perched on the edge of a tiny chair at the edge of the rug.

It is writing time. The program the teacher is using is designed to foster proofreading and rewriting. Everything the children write, therefore, they are urged to reread and revise: look at what they've written, mark if they think it's not right, correct, change. Some children are still learning to write single words; some, like Mark, are up to sentences.

Mark is at the board writing a sentence: "Can catt cach a ratt." (I do not know where he came up with it, but that is his sentence.) He looks at it a moment, decides to make a change: "Can *a* catt cach a ratt." Looks again. Reaches for the eraser, takes a swipe at the "t" in "cat." Hardly has time to smile before he says, "Oh . . ." and lunges at the "t" in "rat ."

Teacher says, hopefully, "Very good, Mark. Thank you." But he is not done yet.

Meanwhile, the class on the rug is falling apart. Derek and LeRoy are grabbing at each other's hands. Jason has curled up for a nap. The teacher is trying to glare them into attention while she watches Mark's operations at the board. Her head is whipping back and forth between the two—encouraging, discouraging, coaxing, correcting.

She is trapped. Mark has the chalk and he is not giving it up. He folds his arms, presses the chalk to his lips, studies his sentence. Crosses out the word "cach," writes "catch" above it. Thinks some more. Crosses out the period. Adds a question mark. Puts the chalk in the tray.

"That's *very* good, Mark . . . Mark?"

Still not done. Unsatisfied for some reason, Mark is back at the board, crossing out and rewriting some more. The teacher gives up watching him, turns her full, furious attention to the disorder on the rug. Children have turned away from the board. They are talking to each other, inspecting their stockings. Two boys are trading shoes. Jason is sucking his thumb, almost asleep.

Mark translates his question into a statement—"A cat can catch a rat."—making all the changes necessary. When he is finally finished, the board looks as confused as the rug. Words crossed out, overwritten, erasure smudges, a glorious mess. Mark smiles. The teacher looks at the board, at him, at her class, at me.

"Thank you, Mark," she says.

I wanted to cheer for him then, on the spot, but I did not dare. The fabulous disruption of his performance delighted me. It seemed perfectly right. I know I should have sympathized more with that woman, out of solidarity as a fellow teacher if nothing else. But I didn't. I wanted to run up and hug Mark for that fantastic act of sabotage.

It was like the wild disorder of Boy Bishop Day in medieval Europe when children took over the civil and religious government of the town, disrupting everything. I want to race through the streets with them. But I also want my shirt collars and cuffs starched and pressed. I buff the tips of my loafers until they shine. When I pose for a photograph, I stand with my feet together. When I organize the courses I teach, I lay out the syllabus day by day, preplanning everything, trying to lock it all in place. Controlling everything. Specifying my purposes and goals. Anticipating problems, trying to defuse them with foresight and ground rules, trying to avoid radical helplessness.

But there is no avoiding Mark or Michael. Children do sometimes take over the town. In spite of my best efforts, they sometimes take over my classroom. One afternoon, Chet Lee looked at Carolyn Hemp and asked her to read her paper to the class again. He completely disregarded me. I had asked Carolyn and a few other students to read aloud to the class, but I had never asked a student to reread. Chet knew nothing of this. He was so affected by her piece on capital punishment—a usually stock subject that Carolyn had transformed by writing about the death-row convict she had corresponded with during high school—that he asked her to read again. She did.

Laurie Litonjua already had the floor one morning in a literature class—she was telling me how much she admired the Satan of *Paradise Lost*—when she turned from me to the whole room.

"Well, who thinks he should have gone back?" she asked. And then she was standing up, balancing her coffee cup in one hand, waving her other arm, scanning the eyes of all her fellow students. "Let's have a vote! How many of you actually think Satan should have gone back to that Heaven, to that God?"

It was a question none of us could ignore. She stood there, waiting, as one by one around the circle the students considered their opinions. And then, because the authority of the moment was hers, she looked at me and demanded my vote, too.

After Teresa Simpson turned in one wonderful paper about growing up, her next essay was a disappointment. She did not give it to me in person, just shoved it under my door without knocking, the title page scrunching up as it slid. Flimsy, insincere, incorrect, too short, too vague—just about everything was wrong with it (she wrote it while battling the winter flu, doped up on antibiotic). Teresa did not even look at me when I handed it back in class, took it without a word, slipped it into her notebook without so much as glancing at the grade. Weeks later, she was in my office to talk about another assignment. I gingerly broached the subject of that D.

"Oh, that?" she said. "I know." She said it almost gaily, running a hand through her red hair.

"I knew it was bad. I told my boyfriend it was. He read it and said it was pretty good, but I knew you wouldn't like it. I even made a bet with him."

It was hard for me to read her smile. This work looked too much like failure to me.

"You made a *bet* with him?"

"Sure," said Teresa. "I bet him twenty dollars you'd give it a D or an F, and you did. And I won."

I wave my badge at students or my detention pad (as I did with those high school boys at Moreau) or my Ph.D. or my words, and sometimes they do not seem even to notice. At times they seem to understand far better than I do just what this thing called school is.

Her first semester at college, Missy Harris was a student in my Freshman English class. We met Monday-Wednesday-Friday at 8:00 A.M. in the basement of Curie. On December 12, I arrived to find the classroom door locked and most of the students sitting on the floor waiting for me.

Whatever it was that possessed me to say it, before I even registered that we were locked out, I announced that today was the feast day of Our Lady of Guadalupe. I had grown up celebrating it. When I was in elementary school at St. Lawrence O'Toole's, we recited a special prayer commemorating the feast. At St. John's College, we hung piñatas off the balcony of the recreation room after dinner and took turns swinging at them with baseball bats.

My students looked up at me, their arms across their knees. Their eyes said, "It's eight o'clock in the morning. We're locked out. What are you talking about? Our lady of who?" Of course, they were right. What had gotten into me? Where did I think I was? Radford is a state university. We don't have feast days. We don't commemorate the saints.

I went off to look for some help in getting the classroom open.

It must have taken me fifteen minutes to locate a janitor

with the right key. When we got back to the hall outside the classroom, most of the rest of the students had shown up. I had already been mentally calculating what to cut from my plans and how best to use the half hour of class time we had left. I was ready to start, but when they saw me the students groaned. They had been hoping against hope that I would be unable to find the key.

"Why don't we just cancel class for today, Dr. Murphy?" someone asked as they struggled reluctantly to their feet.

"Yeah," some others chorused. "It's almost time, anyway."

I smiled: No, no. Work to be done. I have this exercise for you to do. You'll enjoy it (I actually—still—say such things). If I cancel your class, we'll never have time to make it up before the end of the semester. No, no. And besides, I have to give back your journals. Lots of things to do, and we're already behind.

Then Missy Harris spoke, softly but clearly, with perfect timing.

"In honor of Our Lady of Guadalupe?"

I couldn't register at first what she had said.

"How about *that*?" she said. "To celebrate."

Not a glimmer of a smile. She was just offering a suggestion. Since I had mentioned it.

Such moments happen in teaching, sometimes, when our minds merge, teachers' and students', when we understand for a moment the world, school, ourselves. If we do not know fully who and where we are, at least we recognize each other, and at its best that recognition enkindles a sudden, inexplicable joy.

"Why don't we celebrate her feast," Missy said, "by taking the day off?"

It was a gesture of such wit that it felt like grace.

Four years. Can it have been so long ago? The vice-president's voice continues to intone the names of graduates. My eyes race through the list of students in the commencement program. I find Missy's name and listen for it. When she is called up, I lose sight of her behind picture-takers crowding the aisle between me and the stage, but I put the program in my teeth and clap for her.

In a few hours, the lawn will be picked up. By tonight, the families of the graduates will have loaded the last of their trailers and headed out onto Interstate 81 toward home. This time tomorrow, maintenance will have the chairs folded up and shipped back to the rental agency. It will be hard to recall this graduation, to distinguish it from others. Whatever their small surprises, commencement ceremonies blur together like the names, like the years.

In order to remember them at all, I need to fill in the gaps with imagined texture. The only thing left of my students—in this sense alone "my" students—is the story I tell of them. They are the students of my life as a teacher. The work with them that I have been describing here is part memory, part imagination, both anguish and joy. It ends every year at commencement in May with our going our separate ways, begins again every fall, both of us flushed with a sense of fresh possibility. I make it up because I cannot remember enough and because I need it in order to understand myself.

This year as the chairs were being set up for graduation, I walked over to the library to take my books off the reserve reading list. I stopped for a moment on the wide porch and watched the maintenance teams at work. The lawns stretched out before me, sectioned by curving white concrete walks, converging at the circular fountain in the center, bordered in the distance by the brick buildings where I work—Reed, Curie, Young, Heth, Whitt. Suddenly I was struck, as many visitors are, as if I were myself a visitor, by the beauty of the place.

I leaned on the porch railing and looked out over the quad.

A student and someone I imagined was a teacher came down the walk between Tyler and Jefferson. (Was it Missy or Teresa, Craig or John? Who was the teacher?) Both in short sleeves, they walked slowly, their hands in their pockets, talking. There was no ambivalence in their talk. I wanted there to be none. They strolled randomly. It was less than strolling: their path traced loopy curves on the sidewalk, veering toward each other, then apart, one of them walking sideways for awhile, backwards, the other taking quick short steps and then stopping dead in his tracks. It was as if their talk absorbed so much of their attention they didn't have enough left to keep themselves going straight. It was as if their talk so engaged them they didn't care about anything else.

What did they talk about? Wordsworth, perhaps. Virginia Woolf. School. I imagined they were talking about a paper the student had written that had moved his teacher so deeply it elicited memories of her own experience, crystallized her feeling. Maybe the reverse: it was a story the teacher had written. Keep working on it, her student was saying. You *should* write this story, he was saying; I need your story to understand myself.

Perhaps they were arguing—about what it means to be a student in school, or a teacher, about what we do to each other, about the lies we tell ourselves. But if they were arguing, it was with themselves as well as with one another, for they would walk for a while without saying anything, looking down at the concrete in front of them, puzzled. And then they would laugh and both begin talking again at once. I could not hear what they were saying. I am making up their talk, imagining them, telling you once more of my desire.

This is my desire: that in the midst of school they had found or made a way to talk and listen to each other. That they read poems and essays together and brought to their subsequent conversations about that reading something of their deepest selves. That they let each other hear their fear, pride, anger, and hope. That the student learned from their talk to cherish his power to think and speak. That talking with him saved the teacher from cynicism and despair.

It began to rain, as it always does in the spring in Virginia the week of graduation. The workmen ran for the shelter of the trucks. From the cover of the library porch, I watched the two of them walk. Past the empty chairs, along the edge of the lawn, they were oblivious. They had given up staying dry. The rain ran down their faces and arms. I imagined that they recognized their own recklessness. I supposed they intended it. I hoped it was a gesture they were making toward each other, an overture. Nothing matters like this talk, I thought they could be saying to one another. Nothing matters like this moment. It is the best we know; it is the best we are. We have all our day to give to this. We have all our lives.

Notes

Prologue: The Calculus of Intimacy

4 The Carnegie study of college teachers is reported in *The Condition of the Professoriate: Attitudes and Trends, 1989* (Princeton N.J.: Carnegie Foundation for the Advancement of Teaching, 1989).

5 The American Association of Higher Education seminar is described in Diane Gillespie, "Claiming Ourselves as Teachers," *Change* 21 (1989): 56–58.

6 For the self constructed in stories, see Jerome Bruner, *Acts of Meaning* (Cambridge: Harvard University Press, 1990), esp. 111–16.

9 "I am myself": *The Complete Essays of Montaigne*, trans. Donald M. Frame (Stanford, Calif.: Stanford University Press, 1965), 2.

1: New

16 E. B. White, "Once More to the Lake" (1941), in *Essays of E. B. White* (New York: Harper, 1977), 197–202.

2: Lacrimae Rerum

22 James Herndon, *Notes from a Schoolteacher* (New York: Simon and Schuster, 1985), 161, 162.

25 "The chief wonder": *The Education of Henry Adams* (Boston: Houghton, 1961), 55.

30 "Lycidas" : *John Milton: Complete Poems and Major Prose*, ed. Merritt Y. Hughes (New York: Odyssey Press, 1957), 120: 8–14.

Notes

3: His Son the Writing Teacher

42   "Here I was": Susie Murphy, "Postcard from North Yorkshire: A Metaphor for Learning," *Virginia English Bulletin* 39 (Fall 1989): 18–24.

4: Learning to Teach

49   For Bergson on the comic, see Henri Bergson, "Laughter," in *Comedy*, ed. Wylie Sypher (New York: Doubleday, 1956), esp. 66–74.

49   A. M. Bussis, E. A. Chittenden, M. Amarel, and E. Klausner, *Inquiry into Meaning: An Investigation of Learning to Read* (Hillsdale, N.J.: Erlbaum, 1985).

49   "Teaching is trivialized": Lee Shulman, "Knowledge and Teaching: Foundations of the New Reform," *Harvard Educational Review* 57 (February 1987): 6.

50   "More than we can tell": Michael Polanyi, "Knowing and Being," in *Knowing and Being: Essays by Michael Polanyi*, ed. Marjorie Grene (Chicago: University of Chicago Press, 1969), 133; see also Polanyi, *Personal Knowledge: Towards a Post-Critical Philosophy* (Chicago: University of Chicago Press, 1962), 88–89.

51   "What the pupil": Michael Polanyi, "The Logic of Tacit Inference," in *Knowing and Being: Essays by Michael Polanyi*, ed. Marjorie Grene (Chicago: University of Chicago Press, 1969), 142.

57   "I must have recourse": Plato, *The Republic and Other Works*, trans. B. Jowett (Garden City, N.Y.: Doubleday, 1960), 178.

5: Syllabus

64   For the mixed experience of peer–response groups, see Sarah Warshauer Freedman, *Response to Student Writing*, NCTE Research Report 23 (Urbana, Ill.: National Council of Teachers of English, 1987), 161.

6: Personal Essays

72   "Com-position": Josephine Miles, *Working Out Ideas: Predication and Other Uses of Language*, Bay Area Writing Project

Curriculum Publication 5 (Berkeley, Calif.: Bay Area Writing Project, 1979).

72 Ken Macrorie, *Uptaught* (Rochelle Park, N.J.: Hayden, 1970), 20; Macrorie, *Telling Writing*, 4th ed. (Portsmouth, N.H.: Boynton/Cook, 1985), 15–26; Peter Elbow, *Writing without Teachers* (New York: Oxford University Press, 1973), 3–11; Elbow, *Writing with Power* (New York: Oxford University Press, 1981), 13–19.

73 E. B. White, "Once More to the Lake" (1941), in *Essays of E.B. White* (New York: Harper, 1977), 197–202.

75 "Prestige of fact": Paul Ricoeur, *Fallible Man*, trans. Charles Kelbley (Chicago: Henry Regnery, n.d.), 170.

75 Janet Malcolm, *The Journalist and the Murderer* (New York: Knopf, 1990), 71–72, 96.

76 For critical discussion of the personal essay assignment, see, for example, Kurt Spellmeyer, "A Common Ground: The Essay in the Academy," *College English* 51 (March 1989): 262–76; "Two Comments on 'A Common Ground: The Essay in Academe,'" *College English* 52 (March 1990): 329–38; Douglas Hesse, "The Recent Rise of Literary Nonfiction: A Cautionary Assay," *Journal of Advanced Composition* 11 (Fall 1991): 323–33; Joel Haefner, "Democracy, Pedagogy, and the Personal Essay," *College English* 54 (February 1992): 127–37; Kurt Spellmeyer, "A Comment on 'Democracy, Pedagogy, and the Personal Essay,'" *College English* 55 (1993): 89–92; Joel Haefner, "Joel Haefner Responds," *College English* 55 (1993): 92–94.

77 "Producing students": Robert J. Connors, "Personal Writing Assignments," *College Composition and Communication* 38 (May 1987): 179, 180.

78 George Orwell, "Shooting an Elephant," in *A Collection of Essays by George Orwell* (New York: Harcourt, 1953), 148–56; "I perceived in this moment": 152.

79 "The trope of autobiography": Paul de Man, "Autobiography as Defacement," *Modern Language Notes* 94 (1979): 926.

79 For Orwell's posting in Burma, see Bernard Crick, *George Orwell: A Life* (Boston: Little Brown, 1980), 96n.

7: Stories

80 "We mingle truths": Barbara Hardy, *Tellers and Listeners* (London: Athlone, 1975), 4.

83 "There was a darkness:" William Wordsworth, "The Two–Part *Prelude* of 1799," in *The Prelude 1799, 1805, 1850,* ed. Jonathan Wordsworth, M. H. Abrams, and Stephen Gill (New York: Norton, 1979), 4: 124–29.

83 "Wisdom of practice": Lee Shulman, "Knowledge and Teaching: Foundations of the New Reform," *Harvard Educational Review* 57 (February 1987): 11.

83 "What teachers know": Walter Doyle, "Curriculum in Teacher Education," paper delivered at the American Educational Research Association, April 1988.

87 "In Xanadu did Kubla Khan": Samuel Taylor Coleridge, "Kubla Khan," in *Norton Anthology of English Literature: The Major Authors,* ed. M. H. Abrams et al., 5th ed. (New York: Norton, 1987), 1555: 1–5.

8: Failure

90 "What we do": Robert N. Bellah, Richard Madsen, William M. Sullivan, Ann Swidler, Steven M. Tipton, *Habits of the Heart* (New York: Harper, 1985), 66.

11: Symposium

131 "Our knowledge of life": Polanyi, "The Logic of Tacit Inference," 150–51.

135 "For four years": Jacob Neusner, "Commencement Address," Brown University *Daily Herald,* rpt. *National Review,* 12 June 1981: 650–52.

136 "The intense yearning": Plato, *The Symposium,* in *The Republic and Other Works,* trans. B. Jowett (Garden City, N.Y.: Doubleday, 1960), 337; "human nature was": 337.

13: Sursum Corda

159 "What was it then?": Virginia Woolf, *To the Lighthouse* (1927; New York: Harcourt, 1955), 268.

161 "Enlarge my life": Samuel Johnson, "The Vanity of Human Wishes," in *Samuel Johnson,* ed. Donald Greene (New York: Oxford University Press, 1986), 18.

14: Joy

165 "We loved him": Victor Brombert, "A Tribute to Henri Peyre (1901–88)," *MLA Newsletter* (Summer 1989): 3.
167 "Lately I've realized": quoted in Ken Macrorie, *Twenty Teachers* (New York: Oxford University Press, 1984), 161; "I wish I had been": 161; "one class may take": 158.
168 "The form of the desired": C. S. Lewis, *Surprised by Joy: The Shape of My Early Life* (San Diego: Harcourt, 1955), 220.
173 Ricoeur, *Fallible Man*, trans. Charles Kelbley (Chicago: Henry Regnery, n.d.), 161, 170.